SPECTRUM

Language Arts

Grade 3

Dr. Betty Jane Wagner

McGraw-Hill
Consumer Products

Author

Betty Jane Wagner

Professor
Reading and Language Department
National-Louis University
Evanston, IL

Editorial Reviewer Board

Illustration
Steve McInturff

McGraw-Hill
Consumer Products

A Division of The McGraw-Hill Companies

Send all inquiries to:
McGraw-Hill Consumer Products
8787 Orion Place
Columbus, OH 43240-4027

Printed in the United States of America

ISBN 1-57768-473-7

3 4 5 6 7 8 9 QPD 05 04 03 02 01

Table of Contents

Mechanics ....

Usage ....

Special Problems

Grammar ....

Parts of Speech   pages

Sentences

Writer's Handbook

1 Capitalization: Sentences, People, and Pets

At the beginning of a sentence, be sure to capitalize. With proper names, it is also wise.

.... Did You Know? ....

The first word in a sentence is capitalized.

Basketball is fun to play.

Where is my basketball?

The word *I* is capitalized.

Do you think **I** can make a basket from here?

The names of people and pets are capitalized.

Monica **W**ilson is the coach of our basketball team.

Carlos is the best player on our team.

We met **P**atty and **L**isa at the game.

My cat, **B**oots, likes to play with a ball of yarn.

Show What You Know

Read the sentences below. From each pair of words in parentheses, choose the correct word and circle it.

1. (Basketball, basketball) is a fast and exciting sport.

2. In 1891 (james naismith, James Naismith) invented the game.

3. Ted and (i, I) practice our jump shots after school.

4. My dog, (Tipper, tipper), watches us shoot baskets in the backyard.

5. (the, The) Chicago Bulls is a championship team.

6. (michael jordan, Michael Jordan) was my favorite player in the NBA.

Score: _____   Total Possible: 6

Proofread

The paragraph below has six mistakes in capitalization. Draw three lines under each letter that should be capitalized.

Example: today i am nine years old.

    Eight friends came to my birthday party. My brothers, josh and mike, and I planned the party. first we split up into teams and played basketball. Maria made the winning shot for our team. Then we drank gallons of water to cool off. mom knew just what i would want next. she had a big chocolate cake waiting on the kitchen table!

Practice

Write two sentences about what is happening in the picture. Give names to the people and pets.

1._____

_____

2._____

_____

Tips for Your Own Writing: Proofreading ....

Choose a piece of your own writing. Look at the first word of every sentence and all of the names of people and pets. Did you capitalize their first letter?

Now you know how to get your reader's attention: Use capital letters!

2 Capitalization: Places

From Atlantic to Pacific, capitalizing place-names is terrific.

.... Did You Know?.....................

The major words in geographical names are capitalized.

Chicago	**A**rizona	**I**taly
Ohio **R**iver	**M**ount **R**ushmore	**P**acific **O**cean
Lake **H**uron	**A**sia	

We flew directly from **L**yon, **F**rance, to **M**anchester, **E**ngland.

The **R**io **G**rande flows from the **S**an **J**uan **M**ountains of **C**olorado to the **G**ulf of **M**exico.

The names of roads, places, and buildings are capitalized.

Fairmont **A**venue	**H**erald **S**quare
Washington **M**onument	**W**hite **H**ouse

The **S**ears **T**ower is taller than the **E**mpire **S**tate **B**uilding.
Columbia **H**ospital is on **C**entral **A**venue.

Show What You Know

Write the two words in each sentence that should be capitalized.

1. We're planning to take a trip throughout north america.

   _____

2. My mom works at broadview hospital.

   _____

3. My older brother wants to hike through the grand canyon.

   _____

Score: _____   Total Possible: 3

Proofread

The paragraph below has ten mistakes in capitalization. Draw three lines under each letter that should be capitalized. Draw a line through each capital letter that should not be capitalized.

Example: Name a famous Waterfall in New york.

Niagara Falls is one of the most beautiful sights in north america. It is on the niagara river about halfway between Lake Ontario and lake erie. The Horseshoe falls on the Canadian side of the River is 161 feet high. The american Falls is 167 feet high and is in the state of New York. Colored lights brighten the Falls at night.

Practice

Write a paragraph describing something you would like to see on a trip anywhere in the world. Use at least four place-names.

_____

_____

_____

Tips for Your Own Writing: Proofreading ....

The next time you address an envelope, check to make sure that you have capitalized all place-names.

Capital means "important." Do you know that Washington, D.C., is the capital of the United States?

3 Capitalization: People's Titles

Aunt Sarah and Mr. Lu begin their names and titles with capitals, too.

.... **Did You Know?**.........................

Names showing how you are related to someone are capitalized only if they are used in place of or as part of the relative's name.

Fishing is **G**randpa's favorite hobby.
Every summer, my **g**randpa takes us fishing.
Last year, my **m**om caught a huge fish.
This year, **M**om caught only a cold.

Titles of respect used with names of persons are capitalized.

Dr. Elizabeth Blackwell **M**rs. Alvarez
President Clinton **M**r. Peter Tepper

Our class wrote letters to **M**ayor Busby.
Our teacher, **M**s. Whitley, knows the mayor.

Show What You Know

Read each pair of sentences. Underline the sentence that has the correct capitalization.

1. My Uncle has the same name as an American symbol.
   His name is Uncle Sam.

2. *The Cat in the Hat* was written by dr. Seuss.
   He was not really a doctor.

3. In *The Wizard of Oz*, Dorothy called out, "auntie Em."
   At the same time, her aunt worried about her.

4. A main character in *Peter Pan* was Captain Hook.
   He was the mean Captain of a pirate ship.

Score: _____   Total Possible: 4

Proofread

The sentences below have seven mistakes in capitalization. Draw three lines under each letter that should be capitalized. Draw a line through each capital letter that should not be capitalized.

Example: His /Aunt is my grandma Andrews.

Every year, Mom, Aunt Tilly, and grandpa Johnson plan a family picnic. Every year, something goes wrong. One year it rained. My Uncle said that he didn't know he was coming to a swimming party. uncle Theo always jokes like that. One year, I was stung by three bees. One year, everyone got sunburned.

But mom is ready this year. She called the Doctor to find out the best bee sting medicine. She asked the pharmacist about the best sunscreen. She even is taking umbrellas. My Aunt is helping, too. grandpa said, "Your mother and aunt will probably remember everything but the food!"

Practice

Write two sentences about a special family celebration. Use family names and titles whenever possible.

1._____

_____

2._____

Tips for Your Own Writing: Proofreading ....

The next time you write to a relative, make sure you have capitalized all titles of respect when they are used as names or as parts of names.

 You're doing a capital job with capital letters!

4 Capitalization: Dates and Holidays

 "**Y**es, it's true," I say. "Capitalize days of the week, months, and each holiday!"

.... **Did You Know?** ....

The names of the days of the week and the months of the year are capitalized.

Monday	**W**ednesday	**S**aturday
April	**J**uly	**O**ctober

Mai goes to the library every **T**uesday afternoon.
The hottest days of the summer are often in **J**uly.

The names of holidays are capitalized.

Labor **D**ay	**T**hanksgiving	**P**residents' **D**ay

Flag **D**ay is celebrated on June 14.
I look forward to **C**olumbus **D**ay every year.

The names of the four seasons of the year are not capitalized.

spring	**s**ummer	**f**all	**w**inter

....

Show What You Know

Read the sentences below. If the underlined part contains an error in capitalization, circle the word or words that should be capitalized.

We honor Americans who gave their lives for our country on <u>Memorial day</u>. Memorial Day is celebrated on the last <u>monday</u> in <u>may</u>. Some people call
1   2   3
this holiday <u>decoration day</u>. Flowers and flags are placed on the graves of
4
military personnel in <u>spring</u>. Many towns have parades on Memorial Day and
5
<u>independence day</u> to honor people who served our country.
6

Score: _____   **Total Possible: 7**

Proofread

The paragraph below has six mistakes in capitalization. Draw three lines under each letter that should be capitalized. Draw a line through each capital letter that should not be capitalized.

Example: My birthday is in the ~~F~~all on october 9.

Groundhog day is an American tradition that supposedly predicts when Spring will arrive. According to legend, the groundhog comes out of its burrow on february 2. If the sun is shining, the groundhog sees its shadow. The groundhog will go back to its burrow, and there will be six more weeks of Winter. If it's cloudy, the groundhog doesn't see its shadow. The groundhog will stay outside, and Spring will arrive soon. An early spring means lots of blooming flowers in april.

Practice

Write two sentences about different holidays. Use a calendar to find out when each holiday occurs.

1. _____

_____

2. _____

_____

Tips for Your Own Writing: Proofreading ....

Choose a schedule you have written. Make sure you have capitalized the names of the months, days, and holidays. Remember, do not capitalize the names of the seasons.

 Said December to winter, "I get a cap, but you don't!"

5 Capitalization: Titles

Read out loud. Sing out strong. Capitalize titles, and you won't go wrong.

.... **Did You Know?** ....

The first word, last word, and other important words in titles are capitalized.

Book:	Wayside School Is Falling Down
Movie:	Free Willy
Story:	"The Fox and the Crow"
Poem:	"Books to the Ceiling"
Song:	"The Star-Spangled Banner"

Show What You Know

Write each item. Use the rules you know to capitalize each title correctly.

1. "the ransom of red chief" _____

2. james and the giant peach _____

3. rebecca of sunnybrook farm _____

4. the wizard of oz _____

5. treasure island _____

6. home alone _____

7. "mary had a little lamb" _____

8. "over the rainbow" _____

Score: _____   **Total Possible: 8**

Proofread

The paragraph below has ten mistakes in capitalization. Draw three lines under each letter that should be capitalized.

Example: One of my favorite books is <u>Annie and the old one.</u>

    Not another rainy Saturday—we just couldn't decide what to do! Lisa wanted to go to see the movie <u>rookie of the year</u>. Mark was happy to stay home and read <u>the lion, the witch, and the wardrobe</u>. No one wanted to sit around and recite "The Midnight Ride of Paul Revere." We ended up singing old camp songs like "the bear went over the mountain" and toasting marshmallows in the fireplace!

Practice

Make a list of your favorite songs, books, and movies. Make sure to capitalize the titles correctly. Then share the list with someone.

_____

_____

_____

_____

Tips for Your Own Writing: Proofreading . . . .

Choose a piece of your writing that has titles in it. Check to make sure all of the important words have capital letters. If they do not, capitalize them.

 In titles, it's a fact that all important words get capped.

15

6 Capitalization: Friendly Letters

Capital letters are the way to go when you open a letter or you close.

.... **Did You Know?** ....

The first word in the greeting of a friendly letter is capitalized.

> **D**ear Grandpa,　　　**H**i Leah,　　　**G**reetings friends,

The first word in the closing of a friendly letter is capitalized.

> **B**est wishes,　　　　　　　**Y**our friend,
> **T**hanks again,　　　　　　 **S**incerely yours,

Show What You Know

Read these greetings and closings for a friendly letter. Then write the correctly capitalized forms.

1.　dear Mr. Clark,　　　　　　　_____

2.　warmest regards,　　　　　　_____

3.　to my favorite cousin,　　　　_____

4.　yours truly,　　　　　　　　 _____

5.　dearest Aunt Nell,　　　　　　_____

6.　until next time,　　　　　　　_____

7.　very truly yours,　　　　　　 _____

8.　with love,　　　　　　　　　 _____

Score: _____　　**Total Possible: 8**

Proofread

The friendly letter below has two mistakes in capitalization. Draw three lines under each letter that should be capitalized.

Example: I remembered to add "yours truly," to close my letter.

---

4 Pinewood Avenue

Alton, Pennsylvania   18106

June 27, 2000

dear Mr. Spinelli,

    Thank you for signing my copy of your book *Fourth-Grade Rats.* I do have a question. Next year, I will be in fourth grade. How do I go from being a third-grade angel to a fourth-grade rat? Can I be a fourth-grade good guy?

        thank you,

        Larry Cosgrove

Practice

On another piece of paper, write a friendly letter to a faraway friend telling him or her about something that happened to you recently.

Tips for Your Own Writing: Proofreading ....

Choose a letter that you have written. Check to make sure that you have correctly capitalized the greeting and closing.

Dear students,
    Without capital letters for the opening and closing, a letter would be wrong.

        Your teacher,
        Ms. Takes

7 Review: Capitalization

A. Draw three lines under the first letter of the nine words that should begin with capital letters.

last Tuesday, I got a new friend. he weighs about two pounds, has four legs, and has brown and white fur. I named him sport. He is a springer spaniel. Former President george bush had the same kind of dog. His dog's name was ranger. Ranger's mom, millie, lived in the White house. Mrs. bush wrote a book that described life through Millie's eyes.

Score: _____ Total Possible: 9

B. The paragraph below has fourteen mistakes in capitalization. Draw three lines under each letter that should be capitalized. Draw a line through each capital letter that should not be capitalized.

The Panama Canal is a shortcut that ships can take between the atlantic Ocean and the pacific ocean. Before the canal was built, ships traveling from new york to san francisco had to sail around south america. In 1904, the united states paid panama $10 million for the rights to build the Canal. Workers from 97 countries from all over the World helped build the canal.

Score: _____ Total Possible: 14

C. Find and draw three lines under the first letter of the six words that should be capitalized.

I looked out into the audience and was glad to see mom, dad, and my brother, Tom. This was my first time playing in the school band, and my knees were shaking. I come from a long line of musicians: grandpa plays the banjo, uncle Bill plays the flute, and aunt Rita is a whiz on the piano. Our director, mr. Lanzt, held up his baton. I took a deep breath and blew into my tuba.

Score: _____ Total Possible: 6

D. The paragraph below has ten mistakes in capitalization. Draw three lines under each letter that should be capitalized. Draw a line through each capital letter that should not be capitalized.

December 26 is called boxing day in Britain, Australia, New zealand, and Canada. If december 26 falls on saturday or sunday, the official Celebration is always held on monday. On that day, people give money and gifts to Charities, the poor, and people in Service jobs.

Score: _____   Total Possible: 10

E. Draw three lines under the thirteen letters that should be capitalized in the four titles.

Our class earned $100 to purchase books for our classroom library. We voted to decide which books to buy. The two most popular were the polar express and mirette on the high wire. Nine students picked snow white and the seven dwarfs. Only I voted for talking like the rain.

Score: _____   Total Possible: 13

F. Find the two mistakes in capitalization in the friendly letter below. Draw three lines under each letter that should be capitalized.

456 Kingdom Lane
Happy, Storyland 01234
May 24, 2000

dear Cinderella,

There I was happily eating cheese. Suddenly, I was turned into a horse. I had to pull a huge carriage. Please tell your fairy godmother not to make horses out of mice!

your friend,

Mr. Mouse

Score: _____   Total Possible: 2

REVIEW SCORE: _____   REVIEW TOTAL: 54

8 Punctuation: Periods

 A period at the end of a sentence acts like a stop sign.

.... **Did You Know?**.......................

A sentence that makes a statement ends with a period.

> Kevin let the dog out in the wet backyard.
> Blackie tracked mud all over the kitchen floor.

A sentence that makes a request ends with a period.

> Please mop the floor before Mom gets home.
> Leave the dog in the basement until he is dry.

An initial and an abbreviation of a title end with a period.

> Susan B. Anthony   Dr. Martin Luther King, Jr.
> Rev. Billy Graham   Ms. Jane Willis
> Mr. Lee Seung   Mrs. Margaret Watkins

Show What You Know

Read the sentences below. Add ten periods where they are needed. Circle them so they are easier to see (⊙).

Our village held the dedication for a new park last week It is named the

Franklin D Roosevelt Park. Rev John Keats, Dr Suzanne Reed, and our mayor,

Ms Joan Montoya, each gave a speech. Mr Edward M Cameron cut the

opening ribbon. Capt Grooms directed the traffic. Mrs Mabel Keller and

members of her club served refreshments

Score: _____   **Total Possible: 10**

Proofread

This letter has five mistakes in punctuation. Add periods where they are needed. Circle them so that they are easier to see.

Example: Stop at the end.

50 Forest Lane
Fairy Tale Land 43210
June 5, 2000

Dear Mr. and Mrs Elf,

    Thank you for making all the beautiful shoes My husband, Mr Shoemaker, and I sold them. The little outfits in the boxes are our way of thanking you I hope they fit.

Thanks again,

Mrs. Merry M Shoemaker

Practice

Write the names of your family members. Use initials for their middle names and include abbreviations of their titles of respect, such as Mr. or Mrs.

_____

_____

_____

Tips for Your Own Writing: Proofreading ....

Choose a piece of your own writing. Make sure that each sentence that makes a statement and abbreviations of titles are followed by a period.

Yes, it is official. Use periods at the end of sentences, abbreviations, and initials.

9 Punctuation: Abbreviations

Make the days and months shorter. Abbreviate them and end with a period.

.... **Did You Know?**........................

An abbreviation for a day of the week ends with a period.

Monday—**Mon.**   Thursday—**Thurs.**   Saturday—**Sat.**
Tuesday—**Tues.**   Friday—**Fri.**   Sunday—**Sun.**
Wednesday—**Wed.**

An abbreviation for a month of the year ends with a period. The months of May, June, and July are not abbreviated.

January—**Jan.**   April—**Apr.**   October—**Oct.**
February—**Feb.**   August—**Aug.**   November—**Nov.**
March—**Mar.**   September—**Sept.**   December—**Dec.**

Show What You Know

Ramon's soccer schedule has mistakes in punctuation. Add periods where they are needed and circle them. If a day's name or a month's name is not abbreviated, but it could be, write the abbreviation on the line.

Wed July 14	Friday Aug 16	Tuesday Sept 3	Mon October 7	Sat Nov 9	Thurs Dec 19
___	___	___	___	___	___

Sunday Jan 21	Fri Feb 1	Monday Mar 16	Tues April 15	Saturday May 8	Thursday June 28
___	___	___	___	___	___

Score: _____   Total Possible: 21

Proofread

These entries from Mama Bear's journal have seven mistakes in punctuation. Use the proper proofreading mark (⊙) to show where periods should be added to the entries.

Example: Feb⊙16. Today is Wed⊙We are having a Valentine's party at school.

Mar 14. It snowed all day Sat and Sun night. Papa Bear told Baby Bear to go back to sleep. He said all good baby bears sleep all the way through Nov, Dec, Jan., Feb., and Mar.

Apr. 7. Today is Sat, and Baby Bear woke up. She tried to shake Papa Bear awake. He just grunted and rolled over.

July 21. Last Thurs Papa Bear, Baby Bear, and I went for a walk. When we got home, we found a stranger in our house. Baby Bear cried because her chair was broken.

Practice

On another piece of paper, make a calendar for this month and show the days of the week. Use correct abbreviations. The calendar can be used to keep track of assignments and activities.

Tips for Your Own Writing: Proofreading ....

Choose a piece of your writing in which you have used abbreviations for months and days. Make sure you have added periods after each abbreviation.

Shortening the days and months is great, now that you know how to abbreviate.

10 Punctuation: Question Marks and Exclamation Points

✏️ *M*ark *your questions with question marks. Point out your exclamations with exclamation points.*

························· **Did You Know?** ·····················

A sentence that asks a question ends with a question mark.

Have you seen my umbrella**?**

Do you like strawberries**?**

A sentence that expresses strong feelings ends with an exclamation point.

What a good job you did**!**

Help, I'm going to drop this package**!**

···

Show What You Know

Read the paragraph. Change two periods to question marks. Change one period to an exclamation point.

Do you know how the sandwich was invented. It was August 6, 1762, and John Montagu, the Earl of Sandwich, had been playing cards all day and night. Wow, was he hungry. He didn't want to leave the game. Do you know what he did. He told his servant to put some beef between two pieces of bread. Then he was able to eat while he continued to play cards. Ever since, any combination of filling and bread has been called a sandwich.

Score: _____   **Total Possible: 3**

Proofread

There are three mistakes in the punctuation in the report below. Draw a delete mark through the incorrect punctuation marks. Write the correct ones above them.

Example: Have you ever been to Cedar Point. ?

Have you ever hunted for diamonds. Visitors to the Crater of Diamonds State Park in Murfreesboro, Arkansas, do every day. This is the only diamond field in the United States that is open to the public. How can you tell a diamond from an ordinary crystal. Experienced treasure seekers know that diamonds have a slick, oily surface that dirt or mud will not stick to. They keep their eyes open for clean crystals. About 1,000 diamonds are found each year. Wow.

Practice

Write a paragraph to describe what is happening in the picture. Use question marks and exclamation points in the paragraph.

_____

_____

_____

_____

_____

Tips for Your Own Writing: Revising ....

Choose a piece of your own writing. Rewrite some of the sentences to use question marks and exclamation points.

 There certainly is a lot to learn about punctuation!

11 Punctuation: End Marks

Follow the sentence trend! With periods, question marks, or exclamation points, sentences should end.

.... **Did You Know?** ....

A period ends a sentence that is a statement.

> Broccoli is a vegetable that is rich in vitamins A and C**.**

A question mark ends a sentence that asks a question.

> Do you know anyone who likes broccoli**?**

An exclamation point ends a sentence that expresses strong feelings.

> I love broccoli**!**

Show What You Know

Add the correct end marks to each sentence. Circle the periods that you add.

Who invented chewing gum Gum was first used by Native Americans They boiled tree sap and let it dry in the sun This hardened, unflavored sap was called chicle

William Wrigley, Jr., made chewing gum an American favorite What is your favorite flavor of gum My favorite is spearmint gum It's great Wow More than 500 companies make gum today

Score: _____   Total Possible: 10

Proofread

Four of the following sentences have incorrect end punctuation. Draw a delete mark through the incorrect punctuation marks and write the correct ones above them.

Example: Did you know a tomato is a fruit?

Do you know who created Mickey Mouse and Donald Duck! Walt Disney was responsible for making these cartoon characters famous. His company made the first cartoon of Mickey Mouse in 1928? After becoming successful in both films and television, Disney began opening theme parks. Have you ever been to Disneyland or Walt Disney World. They're great vacation spots?

Practice

Write two sentences about the picture. Use periods, question marks, or exclamation points.

1._____

_____

2._____

_____

Tips for Your Own Writing: Proofreading . . . .

Choose a piece of your own writing. Carefully check it for correct end marks. Make corrections where necessary.

Yes, positively! I need an explanation. Is this a statement, a question, or an exclamation?

12 Punctuation: Sentences I

Sentences are hard to understand when the writer doesn't add end marks where they belong.

.... Did You Know?.......................

Sometimes two or more sentences are written as though they were one sentence. The end marks are not placed at the end of each sentence where they belong.

I am taller than Mary Beth is taller than I.

Jerry was playing tennis balls were everywhere.

One way to correct such groups of words is to separate them into two sentences with the correct end marks. Make sure to capitalize the first letter of the second sentence.

I am taller than Mary. Beth is taller than I.

Jerry was playing tennis. Balls were everywhere.

Show What You Know

Draw lines to show where each sentence should be separated.

Example: I have a best friend | his name is Antonio.

Duke Ellington was a famous composer, pianist, and band leader his favorite music was jazz. His band played at the Cotton Club in Harlem that is the section of New York City where Duke Ellington lived. Ellington's band became very popular in the 1930s the band traveled all over the country. Ellington was one of the founders of big-band jazz one of his most famous songs is "Mood Indigo."

Score: _____   Total Possible: 4

Proofread

Use the proper proofreading marks to show where end marks and capital letters should be used to correct four sentences.

Example: Pigs like to eat birds like to fly.

    A terrarium is a tiny earth garden growing in glass I think plants would be very easy to grow this way. The plants inside the terrarium use the same water over and over again they are also protected from pollution. The temperature in the terrarium stays the same insects cannot feed on the plants. Doesn't this sound like a foolproof way to grow plants I'm going to give it a try.

Practice

Write a paragraph about what is happening in the picture. Use different kinds of end marks.

_____

_____

_____

_____

Tips for Your Own Writing: Proofreading ....

Choose a piece of your own writing. Check to make sure that the sentences are punctuated correctly.

Run along to the next lesson to find out more about punctuating sentences!

13 Punctuation: Sentences II

Sometimes sentences run on and on and on and they never seem to stop or do they?

Did You Know?

Sometimes groups of words are put together that belong in two separate sentences. They might be two or more sentences put together without punctuation, or they might be connected with a comma and with the words *and, or,* or *but.*

Incorrect punctuation: This is my pet fish make quiet pets.

Corrected punctuation: This is my pet. Fish make quiet pets.

Incorrect punctuation: These are my cat's kittens that I like to pet and aren't they cute?

Corrected punctuation: These are my cat's kittens that I like to pet. Aren't they cute?

Incorrect punctuation: It is raining, do not let the dog outside.

Corrected punctuation: It is raining. Do not let the dog outside.

Show What You Know

Draw lines to show where each sentence should be separated. Cross out unneeded words such as *and*.

My name is Dumpty Humpty and I had a brother named Humpty Dumpty.

One day Humpty Dumpty was sitting on a wall he fell he had a great fall. I

didn't want Humpty Dumpty to get hurt but he was hurt and he was broken.

Score: _____   Total Possible: 8

Proofread

Use the proper proofreading marks to show where four end marks and capital letters should be added to create correct sentences. Draw a delete mark through two commas and the word *and* twice where necessary.

Example: I like to go to amusement parks and swimming at a pool is also fun.

Do you think that snakes are creepy, slimy creatures, if so, you have probably never met a snake up close. Snakes are reptiles and they are cold-blooded animals, and cold-blooded animals have body temperatures that change with the temperature of the environment. Snakes keep warm by lying in the sun they cool off by hiding in the shade.

Practice

Snakes are very interesting animals. Use an encyclopedia or another reference book to read about them. Then write a paragraph about snakes. Reread your sentences to check for correct punctuation.

_____

_____

_____

Tips for Your Own Writing: Proofreading ....

Choose a piece of your own writing. Read it aloud to check sentences. Correct any sentences that should be separated by using correct end marks and capital letters.

 Correct end marks will put an end to incorrect sentences!

14 Punctuation: Sentence Fragments I

✏️ *A*re sentence fragments pieces of broken sentences?

.... **Did You Know?** ....

A sentence always has at least two parts. One part tells what happened or what is.

> **cut the grass**   **is funny**

The other part tells who or what is involved.

> **She** cut the grass.   **Miguel** is funny.

A group of words that is only part of a sentence is called a *sentence fragment*. A sentence fragment is missing something.

It can be missing the part that tells who or what, or what happened.

> **Fragment:** On the way home.
> **Sentence:** She walked with Alesha on the way home.
> **Fragment:** Rained all day long.
> **Sentence:** We saw a rainbow after it rained all day.

Show What You Know

Read each group of words below. If it is a complete sentence, write *S* on the line. If it is a fragment, write *F* on the line.

1. Yellowstone was the first national park in the world. _____

2. Known for spouting geysers and hot springs. _____

3. The park is located in Wyoming, Idaho, and Montana. _____

4. The park with beautiful scenery. _____

5. You can still see wild bison in Yellowstone. _____

6. See bison in a park. _____

Score: _____   Total Possible: 6

Proofread

There are three sentence fragments in the paragraph below. Draw a line through the fragments. Write a complete sentence for each fragment on the lines below.

Example: ~~On our trip~~. On our trip we saw a huge whale.

   Tomorrow we are going to Yellowstone Park. Because "Old Faithful." I hope to see moose, bears, and wolves. Get there. We are going hiking. After hiking for a few hours. We are planning to stay for a week.

1. _____

2. _____

3. _____

Practice

Imagine that you are on this camping trip. Use complete sentences to write a paragraph about your trip.

_____

_____

_____

_____

Tips for Your Own Writing: Revising..........................

Choose three sentences you have written. Ask a partner to make sure each sentence makes sense by itself. Rewrite any fragments.

 A careful writer never leaves any loose pieces!

15 Punctuation: Sentence Fragments II

If your sentences are falling apart, they may be fragments.

.... Did You Know?..........................

A group of words that is only a part of a sentence is called a *sentence fragment*. Sometimes you can combine a sentence fragment with a sentence to make a complete sentence.

Sentence and fragment: We stayed at the park. Until it started to rain.

Corrected sentence: We stayed at the park until it started to rain.

Fragment and sentence: When Theresa picked us up. We were happy to find dry clothes in the car.

Corrected sentence: When Theresa picked us up, we were happy to find dry clothes in the car.

Show What You Know

Combine a sentence fragment from column A with a sentence from column B to make a complete sentence. Write the sentences on the lines below. Put a comma after the fragment from Column A.

A	B
To see Africa's highest mountain	Kibo is the highest peak.
At about 19,000 feet high	You must go to Mount Kilimanjaro.

1. _____

2. _____

Score: _____   Total Possible: 2

Proofread

Combine two sentences with sentence fragments to make complete sentences. Where needed, draw a delete mark through the periods and add commas above them. Draw lines through capital letters that should not be capitalized.

Example: Tom ran after the ball͵ B̶efore it landed in the creek.

   Until World War I ended. Most American families did not have a bathtub.

Most people did not take a bath every day. Because they did not think it was

a healthy thing to do. Early bathtubs were made of

wood, metal, or rubber. Modern bathtubs

became popular after 1920.

Practice

Add words to make the fragments into complete sentences.

1. **When I grow up,** _____ .

2. _____ **, which is my favorite subject at school.**

3. **Since I want to learn to dance,** _____ .

4. **Last year when I visited my aunt,** _____ .

Tips for Your Own Writing: Revising...................

Choose a piece of your own writing. Read it over carefully and look for sentence fragments. Rewrite any fragments to make them into complete sentences.

Sometimes your mind works faster than your hand. Take the time to write complete sentences!

16 Review: End Marks

A. **There are nine periods missing in the letter below. Use proofreading marks to show where periods are needed.**

7541 Black Oak Ave

Wolfville, Storyland

June 25, 2000

Dear Mr and Mrs Piggy,

    My sisters and I are planning a barbecue dinner on July 10, 2000. We have invited everyone from our neighborhood. Ms Bo Peep, Rev Wily Fox, and Dr Mary Lamb will be coming. Dr Patricia Wolf will begin cooking at 2 o'clock. Please plan on attending. We would love to have you for dinner

        Sincerely,

        Big B Wolf

Score: _____   Total Possible: 9

B. **Use proofreading marks to show where 12 periods are needed in the paragraphs.**

    Have you ever read the poem that tells how many days are in each month? It says that there are 30 days in Sept, Apr, June, and Nov It then says all the rest, such as Dec, have 31 days except one month. That is Feb, which has 28 days in most years.

    There is also a poem that names the days of the week. It begins by saying that Mon has a child that is fair of face. All other days of the week—Tues, Wed, Thurs, Fri, Sat, and Sun—are mentioned. These poems can help you remember how many days are in each month and the names of the days of the week.

Score: _____   Total Possible: 12

C. Add two periods, four question marks, and two exclamation points where needed.

Did you know that sometimes two birds of the same kind look very different The male bird is covered with bright, beautiful feathers Can these bright markings attract female birds You bet they can Why does the female bird have dull, drab feathers Those dull feathers are really a built-in protection Can enemies see her sitting on her nest of eggs They absolutely cannot

Score: _____   Total Possible: 8

D. Delete unnecessary words such as *and.* **Use the proper proofreading marks to show three capital letters, and add four end marks to correct sentences.**

According to legend, the Olympics began in ancient times they were started by a Greek man named Hercules. Hercules and his three brothers ran a foot race and Hercules won the race and the Greeks decided to hold more contests to honor Hercules. The Greeks held the contest once every four years now the summer and winter Olympics take place alternately every two years.

Score: _____   Total Possible: 9

E. Use the proper proofreading marks to correct sentence fragments by taking out unnecessary punctuation. Draw a line through letters that should not be capitalized. Add one missing comma.

1. I think year-round school is a good idea. Because it makes better use of the buildings and staff.
2. When kids take computer classes over the summer. They learn new skills.

Score: _____   Total Possible: 5

REVIEW SCORE: _____   REVIEW TOTAL: 43

17 Punctuation: Commas in Series and Introductions

Your audience will give applause if you use commas to show a pause.

.... Did You Know? ....

A comma follows each item in a series except the last one.

> New York, Philadelphia, and Chicago have well-known city parks.

A comma follows an introductory word or phrase to separate it from the rest of the sentence.

> Yes, Central Park is in New York.
> Before the concert, people waited in the park.

A comma is used to show a pause you would make if you were saying the sentence aloud.

> We planned a picnic in the park, but we had to cancel it because of the rain.

Show What You Know

Read the report below. Add commas after each word in a series.

There once was a Russian who made beautiful eggs for the czar, or ruler of Russia. Carl Fabergé made eggs that were covered with gold silver and other precious metals. Diamonds pearls and valuable jewels decorated other eggs. There was a surprise in each egg. A small golden carriage a diamond-studded flower basket or a royal crown may be found in a Fabergé egg. Today each egg is worth a great deal of money. Collectors own these special eggs, and they seldom offer the eggs for sale.

Score: _____   Total Possible: 6

Proofread

This paragraph on immigrants is missing six commas. Use a caret (^) to add commas where they are needed.

Example: No,I do not like to play soccer.

Between 1880 and 1923, 23 million people came to the United States. Most of these people came from Germany Ireland, Poland and Italy. Many left because there was not enough work in their country. Land in the United States was very cheap and there were many jobs in this country. After arriving in the United States immigrants often settled in areas with other people from their homelands. Areas like Chinatown Little Italy and Greektown sprang up in cities all across the United States.

Practice

On another piece of paper, write a letter to a friend telling about things you would like to do during summer vacation. Use sentences that list things in a series. Use an introductory word like *yes, no,* or *well* to begin one sentence.

Tips for Your Own Writing: Revising ....

Choose a piece of your own writing. Rewrite it by adding names, action words, or descriptive words in a series. Make sure you use commas to separate the words in a series.

Yes, it is true! Using commas can make your writing clear, understandable, and easy to read.

18 Punctuation: Friendly Letters

Sure, it is an open and closed case, because commas in letters set the pace.

.... Did You Know? ....

A comma is used between the city and state in the heading.

Plano, Texas   Eugene, Oregon   Slidell, Louisiana

A comma is placed between the day and the year in the heading.

April 22, 1996   January 3, 1998   November 10, 2000

A comma is used after the last word in the greeting.

Dear Tony,   My dearest Grandmother,
To my classmates,

A comma is placed after the last word in the closing.

Sincerely,   Your best friend,   Very truly yours,

Show What You Know

Add commas where they are necessary.

1. Mequon Wisconsin
2. February 14 1996
3. Dear Uncle George
4. Yours truly
5. To my students
6. With love
7. Sacramento California
8. Dear Luis
9. Grimsley Tennessee
10. Your best friend

Score: _____   **Total Possible: 10**

Proofread

Four commas are missing in the friendly letter below. Use the proper proofreading marks to insert the commas where they are needed.

Example: My favorite aunt lives in New Boston ‸ Michigan.

---

652 Applegate Circle
Lake Zurich Illinois 60047
May 25 2000

Dear Grady

    Thanks for taking care of our pets while we were on vacation. The hike through the Grand Canyon was awesome.

    You can count on me to take care of your dog when you go to hockey camp next month.

                 Thanks again

                 Marietta

Practice

On another piece of paper, write a friendly letter to a friend thanking him or her for a gift or favor you have received. Make sure to use commas correctly in the letter.

Tips for Your Own Writing: Proofreading ....

The next time you write a letter, check to make sure that commas have been used correctly. Add commas where they are needed.

Use commas between the city and state and in a date. Also, use a comma to greet and close.

19 Punctuation: Commas in Dialogue

✎ *To separate who said what in a quotation, commas are the punctuation of notation.*

················ **Did You Know?**····················

When you write a conversation between two or more persons, you are writing a dialogue. Use a comma before and after the speaker's words to separate them from the rest of the sentence.

The teacher asked, "What's round on both ends and high in the middle?"
His students answered, "Ohio!"
Dennis said, "I don't like cheese with holes in it."
"Then don't eat the holes, dear," said Grandma.

Show What You Know

Read the jokes below. Add commas to separate the speaker's words from the rest of the sentence.

1. Julie asked "Why are you taking oats to bed with you?"
2. "To feed my night-mare" answered Bill.

3. "Eat your spinach. It puts color into your cheeks" said Aunt Ellen.
4. Cousin Kyle answered "Who wants green cheeks?"

5. Carley Cat asked "How will I make ends meet?"
6. "Just put your tail into your mouth" advised Melvin Mouse.

7. Paul said "Are there any letters in the mailbox?"
8. "No, they're all in the alphabet" replied Pedro.

Score: _____   Total Possible: 8

Proofread

Use proofreading marks to add four commas to these sentences.

Example: Pablo asked,"When are we leaving for the movies?"

Gary asked "Do you know why a tulip closes up at night?"

"At night the flower feels cold air and closes its petals" said Gloria Gardenia.

Mr. Greenthumb explained "When the warm morning sun arrives, the tulip opens again."

Gloria Gardenia added "You know, tulips also close up on cool, rainy days!"

Practice

Study the picture. Write a dialogue for the two girls talking about a movie. Use commas to separate the speaker's words from the rest of the sentence.

_____

_____

_____

_____

_____

Tips for Your Own Writing: Revising ....

Choose a paragraph from your own writing. Rewrite it as a dialogue using commas to separate the speaker's words from the rest of the sentence.

"Use a comma to separate what was said from who said it," she said.

20 Punctuation: Quotation Marks in Dialogue

 You can mark my words and yours with quotation marks.

.... Did You Know? ....

A quotation is the exact words that someone says. It always begins and ends with quotation marks. Quotation marks look like this: " ".

Marty asked, "Why do elephants have such big ears?"

"Elephants live in hot climates with few trees and need a way to cool off," said Dr. Bell.

The end marks and commas are placed inside the quotation marks.

Marty continued, "I still don't understand how big ears can help."

"When an elephant flaps its ears, it releases body warmth into the air," explained Dr. Bell.

Show What You Know

Read the dialogue below. Use " and " to show where the quotation marks should be used before and after each speaker's words.

That was quite a joke Aunt Angela played on us, said Miguel to Ana.

Ana laughed, It certainly was. I was kind of afraid to open the envelope when I saw that it said there were rattlesnake eggs in it.

I was, too, but we should have known better, said Miguel.

Ana agreed, Yes, we should have known rattlesnakes don't lay eggs.

Right. I really jumped, though, when we started to open the envelope and heard the rattling noise, said Miguel.

Score: _____   **Total Possible: 10**

Proofread

Use proofreading marks to show where four quotation marks are needed.

Example: ⌄No running on deck!⌄shouted the lifeguard.

"I think we should go to Washington for our vacation, Scott said.

The White House is the most beautiful building in the United States, he

announced.

Maura added, "Seeing the cherry blossoms in bloom along the Potomac

River is an unforgettable sight.

Practice

Make up a conversation between you and a visitor from another place. Have each speaker try to convince the other that his or her hometown is the best place to live. Use quotation marks to show the exact words of each speaker.

_____

_____

_____

_____

Tips for Your Own Writing: Revising ....

Choose two sentences that you have written. Rewrite them using quotations. Use commas to separate the speaker's words from other parts of each sentence.

 Remember, when writing people's remarks, use quotation marks!

21 Punctuation: Quotation Marks and Commas in Dialogue

 When writing conversations, use " " to show quotations.

.... Did You Know?......................

Quotation marks are used when a writer repeats a speaker's words exactly. They are always used in pairs. Quotation marks go right before and right after what the speaker says.

"Mrs. Burns left you a message," said Dad.

If the quotation does not end the sentence, you need to use a comma to mark the end of the speaker's words. Make sure the comma is inside the quotation mark.

"I'm going to give Ling Ling a bath," announced Mai.

If the quotation does not begin the sentence, use a comma to separate the first part of the sentence from the quotation. In these kinds of sentences, place the comma before the first quotation mark.

Uncle Henry said, "There's a storm coming."

Show What You Know

Read the paragraph below. Add quotation marks and commas where they are needed. Be sure to place commas and quotation marks in the correct order.

Ms. Carter announced, Today, Mary is going to tell us about something that happened to her.

Mary stood and said "My lamb followed me to school.

Will he make us laugh and play? asked Little Boy Blue.

Score: _____   Total Possible: 6

Proofread

Use proofreading marks where they are needed. Add three commas and six quotation marks.

Example: "That ride was too short," said Scott.

I had been asleep about an hour last night when I heard the funniest little sounds" said Monica.

I asked What did it sound like?

Monica said, "It was kind of like a bunch of little squeaks."

"What was it? I demanded.

Monica exclaimed Winnie had her kittens!

Practice

Pretend that you are talking to your favorite cartoon character. Write your conversation. Make sure to include both the questions and the answers in quotation marks.

_____

_____

_____

_____

Tips for Your Own Writing: Proofreading ....

Find a piece of your own writing. Check to make sure that you have set off the speaker's words by using quotation marks.

When writing someone's words, make sure you keep on track by placing quotation marks at the front and back.

22 Punctuation: Quotation Marks in Titles

Use quotation marks with a story's name. For a poem, use them just the same.

.... **Did You Know?** ....

Use quotation marks around the titles of reports, stories, songs, and poems.

It seems like every year I write a report called "My Best Summer Vacation."

Terrence read his story, "The Day I Met an Amazing Alien," to the class.

I wrote a poem called "The Whispering Pine Tree."

Only use quotation marks when you are writing about the work in a sentence. Do not put quotation marks around the title when it appears on the first page or cover of the work.

Kelly wrote a poem about the weather. She called it "Rain."

Rain
by Kelly Buckley

....

Show What You Know

Add quotation marks around the titles of stories, reports, songs, and poems in the sentences below.

Paul Revere's Ride was written by Henry Wadsworth Longfellow. I called my report Heroes of the Revolutionary War. Cara's report, Betsy Ross and the American Flag, was the most interesting. Yankee Doodle has been a popular American song since the 1700s. The Green Mountain Boys is a story about soldiers from Vermont who fought for the American colonies.

Score: _____   Total Possible: 10

Proofread

Three titles in the paragraph below are missing quotation marks. Use the proper proofreading marks to add them where they are needed.

Example: I called my story ˮThe Mysterious Closet.ˮ

Principal Dodds decided to host a public-speaking contest to help the students of Oak Creek School overcome stage fright. Each student picked a favorite story or poem to recite. Tim Weaver recited the poem Inside Turtle's Shell. Amanda Jones told the Polynesian legend Why Most Trees and Plants Have Flat Leaves. Ted Redwing told a Native American story called How the People Sang Up the Mountains.

Practice

Find your favorite poem. Then write a paragraph telling why you like that particular poem. Be sure to tell the name of the poem. Share your writing with a friend.

_____

_____

_____

_____

Tips for Your Own Writing: Proofreading ....

Find a piece of your own writing that has titles of stories, poems, songs, or reports. Check to make sure that you remembered to use quotation marks.

With stories and poems, both short and long, quotation marks sometimes belong.

23 Punctuation: Underlining in Book Titles

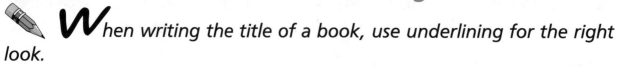 *When writing the title of a book, use underlining for the right look.*

.... **Did You Know?** ....

Printers put the title of a book in *italics* to set it off from the rest of the sentence. You may be able to use italics when writing with a computer.

> Frank L. Baum wrote *The Wonderful Wizard of Oz* in 1900.

When you write the title of a book, you can set it off from the rest of the sentence by underlining it.

> <u>The Wonderful Wizard of Oz</u> is still popular with young readers today.

Show What You Know

Read each sentence below. Underline the titles.

1. Little Navajo Bluebird is a book about a girl who refuses to abandon the customs of her people.

2. Harry Allard's book Miss Nelson Is Missing has a surprise ending.

3. Ramona the Pest is one in a series of books that Beverly Cleary wrote about a girl named Ramona.

4. Ragtime Tumpie is an award-winning book by Alan Schroeder.

5. Tacky the Penguin is an animal fantasy by Helen Lester.

6. Toy animals come to life in A. A. Milne's book Winnie the Pooh.

7. Dick King-Smith tells about an unusual kitten in Martin's Mice.

8. The book The Bracelet by Yoshiko Uchida is about a Japanese-American family during World War II.

Score: _____   Total Possible: 8

Proofread

Read the letter below. Underline the three titles.

Example: I loved reading <u>Iggie's House</u>.

---

136 Sunnybrook Circle
Panama Beach, Florida 36890
October 10, 2000

Dear Aunt Claire,

    I was cleaning out my bookshelf and found some books that Lynne might enjoy. When I was her age, <u>Madeline</u> was my favorite book. Since Lynne is in the first grade, she might like <u>Frog and Toad Are Friends</u>. By the end of the year, she'll be ready to tackle <u>Two Good Friends</u>. I hope Lynne enjoys these books as much as I did!

        Your niece,

        Michelle

Practice

Make a list of your favorite books. Be sure to underline the titles. Share your list with your friends.

_____

_____

_____

_____

Tips for Your Own Writing: Proofreading ....

Find a piece of your own writing that has titles of books in it. Check to make sure that you have underlined them.

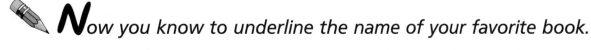 *Now you know to underline the name of your favorite book.*

Lesson 24 Review: Commas, Quotation Marks, and Underlining

A. **Use the proper proofreading marks to add ten commas to separate items in a series in the sentences below.**

The three largest continents are Asia Africa and North America. Africa has many kinds of land, including grassy plains tropical rain forests and the world's largest desert. Nigeria Egypt and Ethiopia have the greatest populations among African nations. In Africa, there are copper diamond and gold mines. Some African farmers grow cassava cocoa beans and yams.

Score: _____   Total Possible: 10

B. **Four commas are missing in the friendly letter below. Use the proper proofreading marks to insert the commas where they are needed.**

712 E. 42nd Street
Albany New York
August 20 2000

Dear Mrs. Kiefer

    Thank you so much for taking our gymnastics team to Atlanta last month. I still can't believe that I saw world-class gymnasts competing in the Olympics. I'm looking forward to working with you and the other team members this year.

                Sincerely

                Kelly McLoughlin

Score: _____   Total Possible: 4

C. Read each sentence below. Use proofreading marks to show where three commas should be used to separate the speaker's words from the rest of the sentence.

1. "Please let me stay up late tonight" I begged my parents.
2. "You know that tomorrow is a school day" my mom reminded me.
3. I explained "This will be my only chance to see the comet."

Score: _____   Total Possible: 3

D. There are eight mistakes in quotation marks and two missing commas in the paragraphs below. If quotation marks or commas are missing, use the proper proofreading marks to add them. If there are quotation marks where they are not needed, delete them.

Heidi asked, Is Dave at practice again?

Yes, he goes to the rink each morning at five and practices for two hours after school each night Dave's Aunt Helen replied.

"Heidi knew Dave never missed a chance to practice his skating." She said Well, I guess Dave knows that practice makes perfect!

Score: _____   Total Possible: 10

E. Use proofreading marks to add six quotation marks around the titles of stories, reports, and poems in the paragraph below.

I called my health class report The Five Food Groups. My dad thought that Eating Your Way Around the World would be a catchy title. Grandpa gave me a poem he wrote about eating called Down the Hatch.

Score: _____   Total Possible: 6

F. Read the paragraph below. Find and underline the four book titles.

I love to read scary books. Some of my favorite books are It Came from Beneath the Sink, Night of the Living Dummy, and Mostly Monsters. My older brother says The Phantom of the Opera gives him chills.

Score: _____   Total Possible: 4

REVIEW SCORE: _____   REVIEW TOTAL: 37

53

25 Usage: Verbs–Do, Have

*How do you do? I **do** fine, but he **does** fine.*

.... **Did You Know?** ....

Each sentence has two parts: the subject and the verb. The subject tells who or what does or is. The verb tells what the subject does or is. The subject and the verb must work together.

Some verbs have different forms depending on the subject.

Do		Have	
I **do**	we **do**	I **have**	we **have**
you **do**	they **do**	you **have**	they **have**
he, she, it **does**		he, she, it **has**	

He **does** his homework in his room.
He **has** a computer on his desk.
I **do** not own a computer.
We **have** to use the computers at school.

Show What You Know

Underline the incorrect form of the verb in each sentence. Write the correct form above.

1. We has a big old house.

2. Dad do the outdoor painting.

3. Mom and Heidi does the trim.

4. The house have ten windows.

5. The windows has many panes.

6. I does the mowing.

7. My brother do the raking.

8. They has a barbecue.

Score: _____   **Total Possible: 16**

Proofread

There are five mistakes in using the verbs *do/does* and *has/have* in the paragraph below. Use proofreading marks to delete each incorrect word and write the correct word above it.

Example: He ~~do~~ the dishes after dinner.
^{does}

We all have red hair. My dad and mom does, my little brother does, and

my two sisters does. My mom and brother has hair the color of tomatoes.

Dad have hair the color of carrots. My sisters do, too. People say I'm lucky

because I has hair that is called "strawberry blond."

Practice

Fill in the name of your community in the blank line of the first sentence in the news story below. Then finish the story. Use *do, does, has,* and *have*.

Today was a big day for the town of _____.

_____

_____

_____

_____

_____

Tips for Your Own Writing: Proofreading ....

Next time you write, use the reminder that **h**e, **i**t, **s**he (**his**) take *does* and *has*. Other pronouns take *do* and *have*.

✎ *The form of* do *or* have *depends on who is having or doing. Check on their forms when you're reviewing.*

26 Usage: Verbs—Am, Is, Are, Was, Were

Verbs are sometimes tricky! But you don't need to be a magician to learn how to make subjects and verbs get along.

.... **Did You Know?** ....

The verbs *am*, *is*, *are*, *was*, and *were* are all forms of the verb *be*. The verb *be* does not show action. It tells what someone or something is or is like.

***Am*, *is*, and *are* tell what someone or something is now.**

> I **am** an artist.   He **is** an artist.   You **are** an artist.

***Was* and *were* tell what someone or something was in the past.**

> She **was** a swimmer.   You **were** a swimmer.
> They **were** all swimmers.   You **were** all swimmers.

Use *am*, *is*, and *was* with *I*, *she*, *he*, and *it*.

> I **am**   she **is**   he **is**   it **is**
> I **was**   she **was**   he **was**   it **was**

Use *are* and *were* with *we*, *they*, and *you*.

> we **are**   they **are**   we **were**   they **were**
> you **are**   you **were**

....

Show What You Know

Write *is* or *are* in each blank to correctly complete each sentence below.

My teachers ____ Mr. Clark and Ms. Juliano. Our school ____ in Fort
                1   2
Lauderdale, Florida. Luis Mendoza ____ our class president. There ____ only
                                   3   4
21 students in our class. Most of the students ____ girls. Mr. Eilert, our
                                               5
principal, ____ the greatest! The teachers ____ pretty cool, too!
           6   7

Score: _____   Total Possible: 7

56

Proofread

There are six mistakes in the use of the verb *be* in the paragraph below. Use proofreading marks to delete each incorrect word and write the correct word above it.

Example: We ~~is~~ on the baseball team.

    Michael Jordan was known as one of the most exciting athletes of the Twentieth Century. He is born in Brooklyn, New York, and grew up in Wilmington, North Carolina. When he was a freshman at the University of North Carolina, he made the winning shot in the 1982 NCAA championship game. He were a member of both the 1984 and 1992 Olympic basketball teams. He are known for his acrobatic dunk shots. Michael are a six-foot six-inch former player for the Chicago Bulls. The Bulls was the national champions of 1996. Michael was now part-owner and president of basketball operations for the Washington Wizards.

Practice

Write a paragraph about yourself and your family. Use the verbs *am, is, are, was,* and *were*.

_____

_____

_____

_____

Tips for Your Own Writing: Proofreading ....

Begin to keep a journal. Proofread your entries to make sure you used *am, is,* and *are* to show present time and *was* or *were* to show past time.

✎ *With the verb* be, *you are sure to go far if you use* was *and* were *when it happened in the past; but in the present, use* am, is, *and* are.

27 Review: Verbs

A. Write the correct form of the verb on each of the lines below.

1. Larry _____ thirty sit-ups every day. (does, do)

2. He _____ them so that he will get stronger. (does, do)

3. He also _____ a set of weights in his basement. (have, has)

4. Lee and Lance _____ a treadmill. (have, has)

5. It _____ adjustable speeds. (have, has)

6. Lee _____ a workout three times a week. (does, do)

7. Lance _____ no time for exercise. (have, has)

8. He always says, "I'll _____ it tomorrow." (does, do)

Score: _____   Total Possible: 8

B. Complete each sentence in the paragraph below by writing a subject noun or pronoun on the line. Make sure your subject works with the underlined verb.

_____ <u>does</u> the cooking at Jeremy's house. _____
₁   ₂

<u>has</u> no time to cook anymore. _____ <u>have</u> a big country kitchen.
                                                    ₃

_____ <u>has</u> a microwave oven, refrigerator, and two stoves.
₄

_____ <u>have</u> big appetites. _____ <u>have</u> dinner at 6:30
₅   ₆

every night. _____ <u>do</u> the dishes.
                        ₇

Score: _____   Total Possible: 7

C. Underline the verb in each of the eight sentences below. Then write *present* or *past* on the line to tell which tense the verb is.

1. Brian Long is a reporter for the *Newton News*. _____

2. The *News* is the largest paper in southern Missouri. _____

3. Brian's first story was about a fire in a factory. _____

4. Five fire trucks were on the scene. _____

5. Fifty people were in the factory. _____

6. Brian was able to report some good news. _____

7. Firemen were able to control the flames. _____

8. All of the people were rescued. _____

Score: _____   Total Possible: 16

D. Each sentence is written to show present time. Use proofreading marks to delete the seven verbs in the sentences below. Add new verbs above each one to show past time.

Mildred Didrikson is an American athlete who was born in Port Arthur, Texas, in 1914. Didrikson is nicknamed "Babe" in honor of Babe Ruth, a famous baseball player.

Babe is a member of the Golden Cyclones basketball team. They are national champions. Babe is a gold-medal track star in the 1932 Olympic Games. People are also proud of Babe's fourteen golf tournament victories. She is the most outstanding woman athlete of the first half of the twentieth century.

Score: _____   Total Possible: 7

REVIEW SCORE: _____   REVIEW TOTAL: 38

59

28 Usage: Verbs–Sang, Ran

I sang while I ran, although I have never sung and run at the same time before.

Did You Know?

Sang and *sung* and *ran* and *run* are pairs of verbs that give some writers trouble.

Sang and *ran* tell about something that happened in the past.

> The Cat Club **sang** in our street until midnight.
> When my angry dad opened the door, they **ran** away.

Sung and *run* also tell about something that happened in the past. They are used with helping words like *have, has, had,* and *could have.* They tell about something that has happened over a period of time or that might have happened.

> The cats **could have sung** all night long.
> They **have run** away, but they will come back.

Show What You Know

Read the paragraph below. Write the correct verb (*ran* or *run*) in each blank.

My mom and I _____ in a marathon race last week. It was the first time
                1

we had _____ a long race. I could have _____ last year, but I didn't think I
           2   3

was strong enough. I _____ the 26 miles in just over six hours. I could have
                       4

_____ faster, but I didn't want to leave Mom behind.
 5

Score: _____   Total Possible: 5

Proofread

If the underlined verb is not used correctly, use a proofreading mark to delete it. Then write the correct verb above it. There are six incorrect verbs.

Example: She <u>sang</u> the same song he had <u>~~sang~~</u> *sung* yesterday.

The Whittier School Chorus <u>sung</u> for our local cable show yesterday. They
1

had <u>sang</u> many times before with no problem. However, this was the first
2

time they had <u>sang</u> on TV. First, Corey <u>sang</u> his solo. He forgot the words!
3 **4**

Mindy and Myra had <u>sang</u> their duet many times before. This time they <u>sung</u>
5 **6**

way off-key. The show ended after the chorus <u>sung</u> the same song three times
7

in a row. They never got the words right once!

Practice

Write two sentences using *sang* and *sung* or *ran* and *run*. Use each word once. Read the sentences aloud.

1. _____

_____

2. _____

Tips for Your Own Writing: Revising ....

The next time you write about something that happened in the past, make sure you use helping words with *sung* or *run.*

If it happened over a period of time or might have happened, a little help from has *or* have *is needed for* sung *or* run.

29 Usage: Verbs—Wore, Done

✏ *I wore my favorite jeans today and yesterday. I could have worn them every day this week.*

.... **Did You Know?** ....

Wore and *worn* and *did* and *done* are pairs of verbs that give some writers trouble.

Wore and *did* tell about something that happened in the past.

Worn and *done* tell about something that has happened over a period of time or that might have happened. They are used with helping words like *have*, *has*, *had*, and *could have.*

I **wore** my raincoat to school today.
I **have worn** my raincoat every day this week.
I **could have worn** my sweater today.
I **did** my social studies report on Chief Joseph.
I **have done** reports before.
I **could have done** a report on any leader I wanted.

Show What You Know

For each sentence, choose the correct verb in the parentheses and write it on the line.

1. The pioneers _____ many new things on the prairie. (did, done)

2. They had never _____ some of those things before. (did, done)

3. When their clothes _____ out, they had to make new ones. (wore, worn)

4. Men _____ hunting shirts made from deerskin. (wore, worn)

5. Women wove the fabric to make the dresses they _____. (wore, worn)

Score: _____   **Total Possible: 5**

Proofread

The note below has five mistakes in the use of *wore*, *worn*, *did*, and *done*. Use a proofreading mark to delete each incorrect verb and write the correct verb above it.

Example: I ~~done~~ my job quickly.
        did

Dear Jenny,

    You won't believe what I done last month. I tried out for a

part in a movie. I have never did anything like that before.

When I tried out, I worn my sneakers. The movie people asked

if I could have run as fast if I had wore dress shoes. Mom told

them I could run that fast even if I worn no shoes at all.

                 Your friend,

                 Enrico

Practice

Write two sentences about the people in the picture. Use *wore* and *worn* or *did* and *done*. Use helping words with *worn* and *done*.

1. _____

_____

2. _____

_____

Tips for Your Own Writing: Proofreading ....

Don't forget to use helping words when you use *done* and *worn*.

 ***A**re you wore/worn out yet?*

30 Usage: Verbs—Gave, Went

Give this lesson a chance to help you with some irregular verbs.

·························· **Did You Know?** ···························

Gave and *went* tell about something that happened in the past.

Given and *gone* also tell about something that happened in the past. Anytime you use *given* and *gone*, you need to use a helping word. *Have, has, had, was,* and *were* are helping words.

Mai **gave** the skates to me.
Van **had given** Mai the skates.
They **were given** to Van by his friend.
Yesterday, we **went** to Sunset Park.
We **have never gone** there before.
We **were gone** before dark.

Show What You Know

Write the correct verb in the blank to complete each sentence.

1. We _____ to the Memorial Day parade. (went, gone)

2. We have _____ to the parade every year. (went, gone)

3. This year, the mayor _____ some soldiers special medals. (gave, given)

4. They had _____ to fight in Vietnam. (went, gone)

5. Many soldiers were _____ medals after the war. (gave, given)

6. Twenty-three soldiers from our village were _____ medals. (gave, given)

Score: _____   Total Possible: 6

Proofread

The paragraph below has four mistakes in using the verbs *gave*, *given*, *went*, and *gone*. Use a proofreading mark to delete each incorrect verb and write the correct one above it.

Example: Last week we ~~gone~~ skating at the park.
                         went

Every day, Old Mother Hubbard has gave her dog a bone. One day, she gone to the cupboard to get a bone. To her surprise, there were none, although yesterday she had bought a new package. Because she had no bones, she given the dog some water. The dog then pushed open the pantry door and found the bones he had hidden. He given one to the cat to eat. Then he ate the rest. Now there really were none!

Practice

Write a thank-you note to someone who has given you something or who has done something for you. Use the words *gave*, *given*, *went*, and *gone*.

_____

_____

_____

_____

Tips for Your Own Writing: Proofreading ....

Make sure you use helping words with *given* and *gone* when you write. *Gave* and *went* do not need any help.

Have you went/gone all out? Have you gave/given your best effort?

31 Usage: Verbs—Ate, Saw

You need a second helping (of helping words, that is!) when you use eaten *or* seen.

······························ **Did You Know?** ·····························

Ate and *saw* tell about something that happened in the past.

Eaten and *seen* also tell about something that happened in the past and are used with a helping word like *have, has, had,* or *would have.* They tell about something that might have happened or that did happen.

The spelling of some verbs changes when they tell about the past and follow a helping word.

I **ate** two oranges and two apples today.
I **should have eaten** some spinach or beans.
I **saw** you eat pizza yesterday.
I **have seen** you pick olives off your pizza.

··

Show What You Know

Write *ate* or *eaten* on the line to complete each sentence.

We _____ very different kinds of food on our trip to Japan. I had
    1

_____ fish many times, but it has always been cooked. We _____
  2   3

something called sushi that was made with raw fish. The Japanese have

_____ raw fish for centuries. They have always _____ different kinds of
  4   5

seaweed, too. On our last evening in Japan, we _____ fish and vegetables
                                                    6

fried in batter. I liked that meal the best.

Score: _____   **Total Possible: 6**

Proofread

Use proper proofreading marks to delete four verbs in bold type that are incorrect. Write the correct verb above each one.

Example: We had ~~saw~~ *seen* that monument last year.

We **seen**¹ the most spectacular caves at the Carlsbad Caverns in New Mexico. I had never **saw**² such large underground rooms. We saw formations called stalagmites that looked like icicles growing up from the cavern's floor. We **seen**³ some that had grown to be more than sixty feet tall. If we had walked farther into the cavern, we could have **saw**⁴ a rock formation called the Bashful Elephant.

Practice

Write a paragraph about the best meal that you have ever eaten. Write about how the food looked and tasted. Use the words *ate*, *eaten*, *saw*, and *seen*.

_____

_____

_____

_____

_____

Tips for Your Own Writing: Proofreading ....

When you use the words *eaten* and *seen* in your writing, make sure you always give them help by using words such as *have, has,* and *had.*

If you have saw the mistake in this sentence, you understand this lesson.

Lesson
32 Review: Verbs

A. **Write the correct verb in the blanks from each pair of verbs in parentheses.**

(sang, sung)

What was I going to do? Baby Lauren wouldn't go to sleep. I _____
1
every lullaby I knew. Then Grandma _____ a song from a commercial on TV.
2
Lauren went right to sleep. Grandma laughed, "I have _____ that song many
3
times. I know it works. Every time Grandpa hears it, he dozes right off!"

(ran, run)

The gust of wind caught Tito's kite and blew it high into the sky. Tito _____
4
over the hill, clenching his kite string in his hand. The kite continued to drift

toward the pond. When Tito had _____ as far as he could, he stopped. If he
5

_____ any farther, he would be knee-deep in water. He slowly let go of the kite.
6

Score: _____   Total Possible: 6

B. **Write the correct verb in each blank.**

1. Mrs. Cain _____ a good job making costumes for the play. (did, done)

2. Mia _____ a dress that looked just like a real queen's gown. (wore, worn)

3. Her red shoes had been _____ in last year's play. (wore, worn)

4. She also _____ a cape Mrs. Cain made from old curtains. (wore, worn)

5. Mrs. Cain had _____ a great job painting the scenery. (did, done)

Score: _____   Total Possible: 5

68

C. Write the correct verb—*gave, given, went,* or *gone*—in each blank. Then write four sentences of your own using each of the verbs.

1. Grandma and Grandpa _____ on a trip to Switzerland.

2. They had _____ to Ireland the year before.

3. They _____ each grandchild a cuckoo clock.

4. No one had ever _____ me such an unusual clock before.

1. _____

2. _____

3. _____

4. _____

Score: _____   Total Possible: 8

D. Choose a verb from those listed below to complete each sentence. Write the correct word in each blank.

| ate | eaten | saw | seen |

I thought I had _____ everything until I went to the Plainfield Pie Eating
                    1

Contest! I _____ some people eating apple, cherry, blueberry, and peach pies.
            2

Others _____ strawberry and banana cream pies. Some people _____ more
         3   4

than one. A few people had _____ pie since six in the morning. I _____ a slice
                             5   6

of chocolate cream pie. Then I saw something called shoofly pie. I would have

_____ a piece, but I usually don't eat bugs!
  7

Score: _____   Total Possible: 7

REVIEW SCORE: _____   REVIEW TOTAL: 26

33 Usage: Adjectives

Use bigger *for two and* biggest *for more than two when comparing is what you want to do.*

.... **Did You Know?** ....

Adjectives are words that describe nouns.

The ending *-er* is added to most adjectives that compare two people, places, or things. The ending *-est* is added to most adjectives to compare more than two people, places, or things.

A coyote can run **faster** than a bear.
The cheetah is the **fastest** animal of all.

If the adjective ends with an *e*, drop the *e* before adding the *-er* or *-est* ending.

large   larg**er**   larg**est**

If the adjective ends with a single vowel and a consonant, double the consonant and add the *-er* or *-est* ending.

big   big**ger**   big**gest**

If the adjective ends with a consonant and *y*, change the *y* to *i* before adding *-er* or *-est*.

tiny   tin**ier**   tin**iest**

Some long adjectives use *more* and *most*.

beautiful   **more** beautiful   **most** beautiful

Show What You Know

Write the correct adjective on each line.

1. We just had the _____ summer in history. (hotter, hottest)

2. Dad was _____ about the weather than we were. (happier, happiest)

3. His roses were _____ than ever. (more beautiful, most beautiful)

Score: _____   Total Possible: 3

Proofread

The paragraph below has five mistakes in adjectives that compare. Use a proofreading mark to delete each incorrect adjective and write the correct one above it.

Example: We picked the ~~bigger~~ *biggest* apples in the orchard.

The larger trees in the world live in the Sequoia National Park in California. The park was created to protect these more amazing trees. Unlike other trees, the giant sequoia's trunk does not get thinner at the top. Some trees are widest than a city street. The taller tree in the park is 310 feet high. The tree called General Sherman is the overall bigger tree in the world. It weighs 6,000 tons and is still growing!

Practice

Write three sentences about the picture comparing the objects that you see. Use adjectives like *busy, loud, quiet, small, slow,* and *happy.*

_____

_____

_____

_____

Tips for Your Own Writing: Proofreading ....

When you are writing comparisons, think of the words *better* and *best.* The *-er* in *better* stands for two and the *-est* in *best* stands for more than two.

 Y*ou couldn't do better if you did your best job on this lesson.*

34 Usage: Homophones–Hear/Here, To/Too/Two

*H*ear! Hear! Here are two homophones that sound the same but are confusing, too—*hear/here* and *to/too/two.*

Did You Know?

Words that sound alike but are spelled differently and have different meanings are called <u>homophones</u>.

Hear **and** *here* **are homophones.** *Hear* **means "to listen to something."** *Here* **means "at" or "in this place." A good way to remember the difference is that** *hear* **has an "ear" in it.**

Can you **hear** it ring?

I am going to put the telephone over **here.**

Another example is *to, too,* **and** *two. To* **means "toward."** *Too* **means "also" or "more than enough."** *Two* **is the number between one and three.**

Maggie and Theresa went **to** the movies and ate **two** bags of popcorn. They drank lemonade, **too.**

Show What You Know

Write the correct homophone in each sentence below.

1. "I'm going _____ the tennis court," Meg announced. (too, to, two)

2. Her younger sister, Peg, asked, "May I go, _____?" (too, to, two)

3. Meg said, "Sure, tennis is a game for _____ people." (too, to, two)

4. Meg added, "_____, you may use my old racket." (Here, Hear)

5. Peg asked, "Do you _____ Mom calling us?" (hear, here)

Score: _____   **Total Possible: 5**

Proofread

Use proper proofreading marks to delete nine incorrect homophones in the story below. Write the correct homophone above each one.

Example: She didn't ~~here~~ what you said. *(hear written above)*

Nick and Alex found an old pirate map and decided <u>two</u> find the buried
₁

treasure. Nick read, "Follow the shoreline <u>two</u> the entrance <u>too</u> the cave."
₂ ₃

The <u>to</u> boys found and entered the cave. "Do you <u>here</u> something?" asked
₄ ₅

Nick.

Alex called <u>to</u> Nick, "I think it's coming from over <u>hear</u>." <u>To</u> furry bats
₆ ₇ ₈

hung from the ceiling above a battered, old chest. Alex took one look at the

bats and said, "I'm out of <u>hear</u>!"
₉

Nick quickly turned and said, "Me, <u>two</u>!"
₁₀

Practice

Write two sentences about what the people in the picture might be saying to each other. Use the words *to, too, two, here,* and *hear*.

_____

_____

_____

_____

Tips for Your Own Writing: Proofreading ....

Remember that *two* is a number for one more than one, and *too* is *too* much, or more than enough.

This lesson teaches about to/too/two homophones in which you cannot here/hear a difference in meaning.

35 Usage: Homophones–Its/It's

✏️ *When you shorten* it is, *you write* it's, *but when it* owns *something, you write* its.

.... **Did You Know?** ....

How to write these two little words, *its* and *it's*, commonly confuses writers.

***Its* is a word that shows ownership. *Its* is a personal pronoun that shows possession.**

The school lost **its** power during the storm.

***It's* is a contraction. The apostrophe reminds you that *it's* stands for the two words *it is*.**

It's going to be out for the rest of the day.

....

Show What You Know

Write *its* or *it's* to correctly complete each sentence below.

1. Listen, _____ the sound of a kitten crying.

2. I hope _____ not lost.

3. The kitten can't find _____ way home.

4. What is _____ name?

5. I don't know because _____ not on _____ collar.

6. Who is _____ owner?

7. Let's look on _____ collar to find out.

8. _____ kind to help a lost animal.

Score: _____   Total Possible: 9

Proofread

Use proofreading marks to delete each homophone in bold type that is incorrect. Write the correct word above it. There are four errors.

Example: ~~Its~~ It's time to go home.

The desert can be hot and dry. A desert plant has to adapt to **it's** climate.
1

A cactus has thousands of widespread roots under the ground's surface.

When it rains, **its** roots quickly absorb water. After a rainstorm, **its** possible
2   **3**

for a cactus to be filled with water! **It's** thick, tough skin helps to prevent the
                                                 4

water from evaporating. A cactus has small, hairy pads on **it's** stem called
                                                                  5

areoles. Thorns, flowers, or new branches grow from these.

Practice

Write a paragraph describing a plant that grows where you live. Use *it's* and *its* each at least once.

_____

_____

_____

_____

Tips for Your Own Writing: Proofreading ....

Review a paper you have written describing something. Check to see that if you wrote about ownership, you used *its,* and if you used a contraction for *it is,* you wrote *it's.*

If its *shows what is owned, then* it *stands alone—no apostrophe. If* it's *is a contraction, then an apostrophe is part of the action.*

Lesson

36 Review: Adjectives and Homophones

A. Write the correct adjective in the blank to complete each sentence.

1. Daryl is the _____ of the three Robey brothers. (taller, tallest)

2. He is also _____ than his brothers. (more unusual, most unusual)

3. Daryl has _____ hair than both his brothers. (longer, longest)

4. This week it is the _____ shade of purple you can imagine.

   (brighter, brightest)

5. Last week, it was an even _____ color. (uglier, ugliest)

6. Daryl has the _____ hair of anyone I know. (stranger, strangest)

7. He's also the _____ guy in the world! (friendlier, friendliest)

Score: _____   Total Possible: 7

B. The paragraph below has six mistakes in adjectives that compare. Use a proofreading mark to delete each incorrect adjective and write the correct one above it.

Alaskan brown bears and grizzly bears are the larger bears in the world. They are easily angered but usually will not attack unless they are threatened. The American black bear is the most commonest species. These bears are fast runners and agile climbers. Asiatic black bears are smallest than American black bears. They are also fiercest than most other kinds of bears. Sun bears are the most small kind of bear. Their claws are more curved and have sharpest points than those of any other kind of bear. Bears spend the day sleeping and the night hunting for food.

Score: _____   Total Possible: 6

C. **Write the correct homophone to complete each sentence.**

1. Dad said I could invite _____ friends to the ball game. (to, too, two)

2. I asked Jonah and Julie _____ come with us. (to, too, two)

3. We all wanted to _____ the announcer sing. (hear, here)

4. He always sings, "Take Me Out _____ the Ball Game." (to, too, two)

5. Driving to the game, traffic was backed up _____ miles. (to, too, two)

6. Finally, Dad reached a parking lot and said, "We'll park _____." (hear, here)

7. Many other cars pulled into the lot, _____. (to, too, two)

Score: _____   **Total Possible: 7**

D. **Write *its* or *it's* on each line to complete the sentences below.**

What swims slowly through the warm tropical water? _____ head is
_1_

like a horse's and _____ tail is like a monkey's. _____ a sea horse! It
_2_   _3_

carries _____ baby sea horses in a pouch until they're ready to be born.
_4_

But _____ not the mother that carries the babies. _____ the father! A
_5_   _6_

father sea horse carries hundreds of babies in _____ pouch. Baby sea
_7_

horses can look after themselves as soon as they are born.

Score: _____   **Total Possible: 7**

REVIEW SCORE: _____   **REVIEW TOTAL: 27**

37 Usage: Regular Plurals

*T*here are plural (more than one) ways to make a word plural!

.... **Did You Know?** ....

A noun that stands for one person, place, or thing is *singular.*

The clown sharpened the huge **pencil**.

A noun that stands for more than one person, place, or thing is *plural.*

The clown sharpened four huge **pencils**.

Add *-s* to the ends of most nouns to form the plural.

Add *-es* to nouns ending in s, ss, x, ch, or sh.

class—class**es**　　peach—peach**es**
brush—brush**es**　　box—box**es**

Change the *y* to *i* and add *-es* to nouns that end in a consonant and *y.*

sky—sk**ies**　　　　story—stor**ies**

Show What You Know

Write a plural noun above for each singular noun that is underlined.

The <u>beach</u> on this island are sandy. Sometimes the <u>wave</u> crash against
　　　 1　　　　　　　　　　　　　　　　　　　　　　　 2
the pier. Many <u>family</u> come here to play in the sun. My family comes here on
　　　　　　　 3
<u>Sunday</u> during the summer. Terri likes to search for <u>shell</u>. She has <u>box</u> filled
　 4　　　　　　　　　　　　　　　　　　　　　　　　　 5　　　　 6
with them. Angela builds <u>sand castle</u>. Dad spends his whole time taking
　　　　　　　　　　　　 7
<u>photo</u> of us.
 8

Score: _____　　　　Total Possible: 8

78

Proofread

There are six incorrect plurals in the paragraph below. Use a proofreading mark to delete each underlined word that is incorrect and write the correct plural above it.

Example: He is listening to ~~storys~~ ^{stories} on the radio.

Jeremy has two <u>gardenes</u> in his yard. In one garden, he grows <u>petuniaes</u>
1 2

and <u>daisies</u>. In the other, he grows <u>carrotes</u> and <u>beanes</u>. There are raspberry
3 4 5

<u>bushs</u> along the edge of the garden. Yesterday, Jeremy picked <u>bunchs</u> of
6 7

fresh, green spinach for dinner.

Practice

Write a paragraph describing what is happening in the picture. Use plural nouns.

_____

_____

_____

_____

_____

_____

Tips for Your Own Writing: Proofreading ....

When you write plural forms, be sure to add -es to words that end in *sh*, *ch*, *s*, *ss*, and *x*, and always change the *y* to *i* before you add -es to make plural words that end in a consonant and *y*.

***W**ith these simple rules, you don't have to rely on hunches to make most words plural.*

38 Usage: Irregular Plurals

✏️ *Just when you think you know all the rules about making plurals, you'll find there are words that don't follow the rules.*

·························· **Did You Know?** ···························

There are some nouns that do not follow the rules for most plural nouns.

Some nouns have irregular plural forms. These plural nouns do not follow a pattern, so you just have to memorize them.

woman—women	man—men	child—children
foot—feet	goose—geese	ox—oxen
mouse—mice	tooth—teeth	cactus—cacti

For some nouns, the singular and plural forms are the same.

deer—deer	moose—moose	trout—trout
sheep—sheep	series—series	salmon—salmon

··

Show What You Know

Read the following sentences. Write the singular form above each underlined word.

Dad and Uncle Glen are taking a <u>series</u> of fishing classes. They want to
                                      1
learn how to catch <u>salmon</u>. Last month they went on a fishing trip with
                      2
several other <u>men</u>. Uncle Glen caught five <u>trout</u>. His <u>feet</u> were cold from
                3   **4**   **5**
standing in the stream for hours. Dad didn't catch anything but two <u>mice</u> in
                                                                      6
his tent!

Score: _____   **Total Possible: 6**

Proofread

There are four incorrect plurals in the paragraph below. Use a proofreading mark to delete each underlined word that is incorrect and write the correct plural above it.

Example: Mary lost two ~~tooths~~ ^{teeth} last night.

Mom invited four <u>womans</u> out to the farm for a picnic. Each one brought
1

her <u>childs</u>. One child wanted to feed the <u>sheep</u>. Another wanted to pet the
2   3

<u>gooses</u>. The littlest child dangled his <u>foots</u> in the pond.
4   5

Practice

Write a paragraph that tells about the picture. Use the plural forms of nouns when you can.

_____

_____

_____

_____

_____

_____

Tips for Your Own Writing: Proofreading ....

Sometimes when you write a plural, the word you write does not look right. Keep a dictionary handy to check the spelling of the plural form. Dictionaries show the singular form in bold type and then show the plurals if they are irregular.

 Don't get cold feet/foots about forming irregular plurals.

39 Usage: Singular Possessives

Singular nouns take apostrophe s ('s) when they show that the noun has or owns something.

························· **Did You Know?** ····························

A possessive noun shows ownership or a relationship between two things. An apostrophe (') is always used to mark possessive nouns.

Jane**'s** mountain bike is red.
The windowsill is the cat**'s** favorite place to sleep.

A singular possessive noun shows ownership by one person or thing.

Gary**'s** locker   the principal**'s** office

To make a singular noun possessive, just add 's.
the smile of the baby—the baby**'s** smile

Show What You Know

On each line below, write the possessive form of the word in parentheses.

1. This is the house that Jack built. Is this _____ house? (Jack)

2. Mary has a garden. How does _____ garden grow? (Mary)

3. Little Boy Blue, come blow your horn. The _____ flute broke. (girl)

4. Jack jumped over the candlestick. Did the _____ flame hurt? (candle)

5. A wise old owl lived in an oak. Is the tree really the _____ home? (owl)

6. Little Miss Muffet sat on a tuffet. Where was the _____ chair? (girl)

Score: _____   Total Possible: 6

Proofread

Read the paragraph below. There are three apostrophes missing. Use the proper proofreading marks to add an apostrophe to words that show possession.

Example: We are going to Alisha's house after school.

Dad can't find his car keys. He thinks he may have left them in Grandpas truck. I think he dropped them near Grandmas rosebushes. He has another set of keys, but they are in his boss's car. I said, "Let's look in Moms purse. You can find anything in there!"

Practice

The animals are having a garage sale to raise money for a new park. Write a paragraph about what each animal has brought to sell. Use singular possessive nouns when you can.

_____

_____

_____

_____

_____

Tips for Your Own Writing: Proofreading ....

Do not confuse plurals and possessives that sound alike, like *dads* and *Dad's*. Remember to use the apostrophe *s* to make the noun possessive.

 When a singular noun is possessive, add a simple 's to it.

40 Usage: Singular and Plural Possessives

 Possessives help you hold your own.

···························· **Did You Know?** ····························

A singular possessive noun shows ownership by one person or thing.

the **ship's** captain   the **sailor's** uniform

A plural possessive noun shows ownership by more than one person or thing.

the **cities'** streets   the **states'** governors

To make a plural noun that ends in *s* a possessive noun, add only the apostrophe.

girls—girls'   schools—schools'

To make a plural noun that does not end in *s* a possessive noun, add an apostrophe and *s*.

children—children**'s**   teeth—teeth**'s**

Show What You Know

Change the underlined words to include a plural possessive noun. The first one is done for you.

1. The cameras show the <u>faces of the sea otters</u>.
   sea otters' faces

2. Otters sometimes play by sliding down the <u>slopes of the riverbanks</u>.

3. The <u>mother of pups</u> watches them as they play.

4. The mother otter cracks open the <u>shells of sea urchins</u> for food.

5. She grooms the <u>coats of the babies</u> to keep them clean and waterproof.

Score: _____   Total Possible: 4

Proofread

Read the paragraph below. There are four apostrophes and one apostrophe _s_ missing. Use proper proofreading marks to show where they should be added.

Example: The men's tennis match is tomorrow.

During the monthly teachers meeting, Principal Clark announced that the district would hold an all-schools' camp out on May 24. Highview School would pitch tents in the park. Well, this idea certainly grabbed the students attention! The boys campsite would be out near the playground, and the girls area would be next to the tennis courts. There would be more than 400 kids in the park. Some of the children parents would be there, too!

Practice

Write a paragraph to describe what is happening in the picture. Use both singular and plural possessive nouns.

_____

_____

_____

_____

_____

Tips for Your Own Writing: Proofreading ....

When you write plural possessives, you usually add only an apostrophe unless you have a plural that does not end in _s_, and then you add an apostrophe _s_.

 Children's, _not_ childrens', _is the correct plural possessive._

41 Usage: Plurals and Possessives

 Is it a plural or a possessive? Let the apostrophe be your guide.

.... Did You Know? ....

People are sometimes confused by possessives and plurals because the two forms sound alike, but they are written differently. The possessive form always has an apostrophe. The apostrophe is the signal that means ownership.

Jeremy collects old *coins.* (plural)
Jeremy's collection was at the library. (singular possessive)
The *coins'* value increases every year. (plural possessive)

Show What You Know

Read each sentence. If the underlined word means more than one, write *plural* on the line. If it shows ownership, write *possessive*.

1. <u>Millions</u> visit the Grand Canyon yearly. _____

2. Most of them view the canyon from one of the <u>rims</u>. _____

3. The <u>canyon's</u> walls show layers of rock. _____

4. The <u>earth's</u> forces and erosion formed the Grand Canyon. _____

5. Guides can answer <u>hikers'</u> questions. _____

6. The <u>Colorado River's</u> rapids provide exciting raft trips. _____

7. There are many different <u>trails</u> inside the canyon. _____

8. Beautiful, clear-blue <u>waterfalls</u> roar down the sides of the canyon. _____

Score: _____   Total Possible: 8

Proofread

Use proofreading marks to delete three mistakes in plural and possessive forms in the note below. Write the correct word above each mistake.

Example: The ~~runner's~~ ^{runners} are in place.

Dear Mr. Cirrillo,

    Ted and I really enjoyed going to the rodeo. I liked the

bucking broncos' best. The riders skills were awesome. Ted

liked the rodeo clowns. Thanks for one of summers great

memories!

                          Sincerely,

                          Brian West

Practice

Write a paragraph describing the animals in the picture. Use both plural and possessive nouns.

_____

_____

_____

_____

_____

Tips for Your Own Writing: Proofreading ....

If you are not sure whether a word is a plural or a possessive, look to see if a noun comes right after the word. If it does, the word is probably possessive.

 A possessive noun must own something.

42 Usage: Contractions with *Not*

✎ *A* contraction is one word that was once two. When you make a contraction, you squeeze together (or contract) the two words into one.

························ **Did You Know?** ·····························

A contraction is a shortened form of two words that are joined together. When the words are contracted, some letters are left out. An apostrophe takes the place of the letters that have been left out.

My bicycle **does not** work.   My bicycle **doesn't** work.

Many contractions are made by putting together a verb and the word *not*.

did not—did**n't**	are not—are**n't**
do not—do**n't**	was not—was**n't**
have not—have**n't**	could not—could**n't**
has not—has**n't**	should not—should**n't**

Two exceptions are:

cannot—ca**n't**   will not—wo**n't**

Show What You Know

Write a contraction above the underlined words in each sentence.

We <u>are not</u> smiling. The car <u>will not</u> start, and the mechanic <u>cannot</u> fix it
  1   2   3
until Friday. Antonia <u>could not</u> go to her piano lesson. Raphael <u>was not</u> able
                           4   5
to go to baseball practice. I <u>have not</u> gone to the library to work on my
                                  6
report. We probably <u>should not</u> blame "Old Betsy."
                         7

Score: _____   Total Possible: 7

Proofread

There are five mistakes in contractions in the note below. Use the proper proofreading marks to add apostrophes where they are needed.

Example: They haven't come outside yet.

Dear Teresa,

I wont be home from work until 7:30 tonight. Dad cant make it home early either. Carlito doesnt have a soccer game today, so he will be home at about 4:00. Why dont you finish your homework together? I didnt plan anything for dinner, so we will order pizza when I get home.

Love,

Mom

Practice

On another piece of paper, write a letter to a company telling them what you think about one of their products. Describe what you like and dislike about the product.

Tips for Your Own Writing: Proofreading ....

Contractions are like shortcuts. You cannot take the shortcut without using an apostrophe. Check your contractions.

*W*on't *is a special contraction. It is formed from the words* will *and* not *but is not "willn't."*

43 Usage: Contractions with *Am*, *Have*, *Will*, *Is*, and *Are*

 Contractions are a kind of shortcut. Two words are shortened into one.

·· **Did You Know?** ·····························

Some contractions are formed by joining the words I, *you, she, he, it, we,* or *they* with a verb.

I + am = I'm
I + have = I've
he + is = he's
she + is = she's
it + is = it's
she + will = she'll

we + are = we're
we + have = we've
you + are = you're
they + are = they're
they + will = they'll

Show What You Know

Write the letter of the words in Column B that matches the contraction in Column A.

Column A	Column B
_____ **1.** I'm	**a.** you are
_____ **2.** they're	**b.** I have
_____ **3.** you're	**c.** we are
_____ **4.** I've	**d.** it is
_____ **5.** we're	**e.** they are
_____ **6.** it's	**f.** she will
_____ **7.** she'll	**g.** I am

Score: _____   Total Possible: 7

Proofread

Read the following paragraph. Use proofreading marks to delete four incorrect contractions and write the correct contraction above each one.

Example: My sister thinks ~~shes~~ *she's* going to the ball game.

Wev'e got tickets to the ice show. You'll be amazed at how the skaters seem to fly over the ice. Ive never seen professional skaters before. My brother plays hockey and he'is a great fan of all ice sports. He'll really appreciate the skaters' skills. He thinks theyll combine both power and style.

Practice

Read about an athlete or another person you admire. Write a paragraph telling about why you admire the person. Use contractions to make your writing sound more natural.

_____

_____

_____

_____

_____

Tips for Your Own Writing: Proofreading ....

If you are not sure about where to place the apostrophe, think about the two words that the contraction replaces. Then make sure you place the apostrophe where the letters are missing.

 It's a fact! You need an apostrophe when words contract.

44 Review: Plurals, Possessives, Contractions

A. Write the plural form of each word on the lines below.

1. journey _____

2. brush _____

3. box _____

4. puppy _____

5. baby _____

6. surprise _____

7. beach _____

8. glass _____

Score: _____   Total Possible: 8

B. Write the plural form of each word on the lines below.

1. woman _____

2. tooth _____

3. man _____

4. goose _____

5. mouse _____

6. deer _____

7. child _____

8. moose _____

Score: _____   Total Possible: 8

C. Add an apostrophe to the four boldface words that show ownership.

A tornado swept through the **streets** of the city last night. A **buildings**
                              1   2
roof was peeled away. The big oak **trees** leaves were pulled from its
                                   3
branches. Many **cars** were turned over. The **citys** water supply was cut off.
                4   5
Some **roads** were closed. The **librarys** windows were shattered.
      6   7

Score: _____   Total Possible: 4

92

D. Rewrite each of the following phrases on the lines, using a plural possessive.

1. the names of the countries _____

2. the products of the regions _____

3. the crops of the farmers _____

4. the jobs of the workers _____

Score: _____   Total Possible: 4

E. Circle the correct form of the word in each sentence below.

The (teams, teams') were ready to race. Each (schools, school's) team
                1   2
wore a different color. The (runners, runner's) began to line up. Where were
                                        3
(Rosas, Rosa's) shoes? (Whistles, Whistle's) began to blow!
    4   5

Score: _____   Total Possible: 5

F. Read each sentence below. On the lines below, write the two words that make up each of the four underlined contractions.

1. Some people don't follow basic safety rules. _____

2. Children shouldn't play on busy streets. _____

3. Jim didn't look both ways before crossing the highway. _____

4. Aaron wasn't wearing his seat belt. _____

Score: _____   Total Possible: 4

G. Write the contraction for the underlined words above each.

I have invited ten friends to a pizza party. We will order pizza. We are
    1   2   3
going to eat outside. It is nice to finally have warm weather.
                        4

Score: _____   Total Possible: 4

REVIEW SCORE: _____   REVIEW TOTAL: 37

45 Usage: Regular Verb Tense

*V*erbs change to show the past because today becomes yesterday so fast.

.... **Did You Know?** ....

Tense is a word that means "time." The tense of a verb tells you when the action takes place.

A verb in the *present tense* shows action that happens now.

The soccer players **kick** the ball toward the net.

A verb in the *past tense* shows action that already happened. Add *-ed* to form the past tense of most verbs.

The soccer players **kicked** the ball toward the net.

To form the past tense of verbs that end in *e*, drop the *e* and add *-ed.*

rake—rak**ed**   place—plac**ed**   taste—tast**ed**

Show What You Know

Write the past tense of the verb in parentheses.

1. We _____ to the movies. (walk)

2. We didn't know that Len's dog _____ us. (follow)

3. We didn't notice that people _____ at us. (point)

4. We finally _____ around. (turn)

5. Skipper _____ a dollar bill in his mouth. (carry)

Score: _____   **Total Possible: 5**

Proofread

There are four mistakes in verb tense in the paragraph below. Use proper proofreading marks to add *-ed* to show action that has already happened. In one mistake, you must drop an *e* before you add the *-ed*.

Example: He tast~~e~~ ^{ed} lobster for the first time yesterday.

In 1497, Amerigo Vespucci sail to a new land. He call it *Mundus Novus,* which means "New World" in Latin. Many years later, a German geographer decide to name the new land *America* after Amerigo Vespucci. The new land was South America. Later, North America, where Viking explorers first land in about A.D. 1000, was also named after Amerigo Vespucci.

Practice

Write a paragraph about an explorer you know about. When you are finished writing, reread your paragraph to check for the proper spelling of past tense verbs.

_____

_____

_____

_____

_____

Tips for Your Own Writing: Proofreading ....

Make sure that if you write about something that has already happened, you use the past tense of the verbs.

 Don't let verbs make you tense!

46 Usage: Irregular Verb Tense

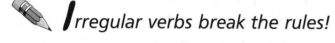
Irregular verbs break the rules!

.... **Did You Know?** ....

Some verbs are special. They do not end in -*ed* to show past time. These verbs are called *irregular verbs* because they do not follow the pattern for forming the past tense. They have one special spelling to show past time.

Erica **takes** us to the city each month. (present)
Last month, she **took** us to the art museum. (past)
We usually **ride** the train to the city. (present)
On our last trip, we **rode** the bus. (past)

Other irregular verbs include:

break—broke	begin—began	come—came
do—did	draw—drew	eat—ate
make—made	think—thought	write—wrote
say—said	catch—caught	run—ran
grow—grew	win—won	give—gave
spring—sprung	buy—bought	

Show What You Know

Write the past tense of the verb over each underlined irregular verb in the sentences below.

Julio <u>run</u> in a 5K race last week. He <u>think</u> that he would win. Tanya <u>come</u>
  ¹   ²   ³

from behind and <u>catch</u> up with Julio. Tanya passed him and <u>win</u> the race. She
                  ⁴   ⁵

<u>break</u> the school record. Julio <u>do</u> not feel bad about losing the race. He <u>say</u> he
 ⁶   ⁷   ⁸

will try harder next time.

Score: _____   Total Possible: 8

Proofread

Read the paragraph below. Use proofreading marks to delete six incorrect verbs in the sentences and write the correct verb above each one.

Example: Todd ~~catch~~ caught the biggest fish.

Last year, Samantha grow pumpkins in the garden. She give one to Linda.

Linda take the pumpkin home. She drew a face on the pumpkin. Her mom

make a pumpkin pie. Linda eat the seeds. Then she write Samantha a thank-

you note.

Practice

You have a green thumb and your vegetables are huge! Write a paragraph about your garden. Use the past tense of *grow, give, spring, begin,* and *buy*.

_____

_____

_____

_____

_____

Tips for Your Own Writing: Proofreading ....

Saying the past tense aloud can help you decide whether the verb takes *-ed* to form the past tense or is irregular. *Sitted* just does not sound right!

If you are not sure about the past tense of a verb, look it up in a dictionary.

47 Usage: Verb Agreement

Do you ever wear a winter coat and a bathing suit together? Parts of a sentence have to "go together" just as your clothes do.

.... **Did You Know?** ....

The verb has to agree with the subject of the sentence. This means that they must both be either singular or plural.

Usually if the subject is singular, or the pronoun *he, she,* **or** *it,* **add** *-s* **or** *-es* **to the verb.**

> Dad **remembers** when few homes had TV sets.
> He often **reads** to the class.

If the subject is more than one, or the pronoun *I, you, we,* **or** *they,* **do** <u>not</u> **add** *-s* **or** *-es* **to the verb.**

> My parents always **watch** the news on TV.
> I **ride** my bike to school.

Show What You Know

Write the verb on the line that correctly completes each sentence.

1. Adam _____ on the new computer. (works, work)

2. He _____ it to do his homework. (use, uses)

3. His brothers _____ games on it. (plays, play)

4. His mom _____ stories on it. (writes, write)

5. His sister _____ reports for school. (type, types)

6. Computers _____ many jobs easier. (makes, make)

Score: _____   **Total Possible: 6**

Proofread

Read the paragraph below. There are five mistakes in subject-verb agreement. Use a proofreading mark to delete each incorrect word and write the correct word above it.

Example: Jessica ~~talk~~ on the phone too long.
talks

    The birth of a baby elephant at the zoo is an exciting event. Soon after it is born, the baby wobble to its feet. Its mother nudge it to take its first steps. The thirsty baby drink its mother's milk. The older elephants stroke it with their trunks to welcome it to the herd. Mama elephant teach it to use its trunk to drink and grab food. She even show it how to squirt showers of water over itself.

Practice

Add verbs to sentences 1 and 3. Add subjects to sentences 2 and 4. Make sure each subject and verb work together.

1. Mountain hikers _____.

2. _____ appears in the distance.

3. A family of bears _____.

4. _____ block the trail.

Tips for Your Own Writing: Proofreading ....

Let your ears be the judge of whether the parts of the sentence agree with each other. Read what you write out loud.

 Subjects and verbs should always agree.

Lesson 48 Review: Verbs

A. **Each sentence shows present time. Use proofreading marks to change the eight underlined verbs to show past time. Write the past tense of the verb above each underlined word.**

Officer Jane comes to speak to our class. She brings safety posters. She
1   2

talks about bicycle and playground safety. She helps us write some safety
3   4

rules of our own. Our teacher shows us a film about school bus safety.
                                                                      5

Then we tour the police station. We ask Captain Jarvis about traffic safety. He
        6   7

offers us a ride in his police car.
8

                                       Score: _____   **Total Possible: 8**

B. **Write the correct verb to complete each sentence.**

1. Astronauts often _____ up in space today. (go, went)

2. Some people once _____ space travel was impossible. (think, thought)

3. In the 1960s, Neil Armstrong _____ in *Apollo II.* (fly, flew)

4. He actually _____ on the surface of the moon. (stand, stood)

5. He _____ moon rocks back to Earth. (bring, brought)

6. Reporters _____ many stories about the lunar landing. (write, wrote)

7. Millions of Americans _____ the moon landing on TV. (see, saw)

8. Today astronauts no longer _____ to the moon. (fly, flew)

9. Now they _____ the space shuttle to and from space. (take, took)

                                       Score: _____   **Total Possible: 9**

C. Write the past tense of each verb on the line.

1. The itsy-bitsy spider climb up the water spout.   _____

2. Down come the rain.   _____

3. It wash the spider out.   _____

4. Out come the sun.   _____

5. It dry up all the rain.   _____

6. The itsy-bitsy spider crawl up the spout again.   _____

Score: _____   Total Possible: 6

D. Write the correct form of the word in parentheses to complete each sentence.

1. The bus _____ late this morning. (is, are)

2. We _____ at the corner. (wait, waits)

3. Dad _____ to drive us to school. (offers, offer)

4. The traffic signal _____ on the highway. (breaks, break)

5. We _____ the bus at the last minute. (boards, board)

6. Our teacher, Ms. Kerr, _____ outside. (waits, wait)

Score: _____   Total Possible: 6

E. Write a present tense verb that agrees with each subject.

1. (to buy)   She _____   **4.** (to wear) He _____

2. (to see)   I _____   **5.** (to carry) They _____

3. (to cry)   Bill _____   **6.** (to lean) It _____

Score: _____   Total Possible: 6

REVIEW SCORE: _____   REVIEW TOTAL: 35

49 Usage: Subject-Pronoun Agreement

What do pronouns replace? They replace nouns or other pronouns.

.... **Did You Know?** ....

A pronoun is a word that can take the place of one or more nouns or pronouns in a sentence.

Franklin was a printer. **He** was also a writer.

Subject pronouns are used as subjects in a sentence. Subjects are the persons or things that do whatever is being done in the sentence.

I, you, he, she, and it are subject pronouns that mean only one.

I saw Henri. **He** was with Sam.

You, we, and they are subject pronouns that mean more than one.

Jill and I are friends. **We** are close.

When you use I with another noun or pronoun, you should put I last.

Liu and **I** went to the library.

Show What You Know

Read each sentence below. Circle the five subject pronouns.

What do you know about Sally Ride? She was the first female astronaut in the U.S. space program. In 1983 Sally rocketed into space on a space shuttle. It was named *Challenger*. She and John Fabian operated the shuttle's robotic arm. They used it to launch and retrieve satellites.

Score: _____   **Total Possible: 5**

Proofread

On the line, write a pronoun to take the place of the underlined word or words in each sentence.

Example: <u>John</u> worked on the committee, and ____he____ also decorated.

    <u>Kyle and Karen</u> wanted to earn money because _____ wanted to go to

1

summer camp. <u>Kyle</u> made flyers, and _____ gave the flyers to all the

2

neighbors. <u>The flyers</u> read: "Lawn Mowing, $6 each yard," and _____

3

listed Kyle's phone number. <u>Mr. Karres, Ms. Blumberg, and I</u> called the

number on the flyers, and _____ asked Kyle to mow our lawns. Later, I

4

saw the <u>flyer</u> Karen made, and _____ read: "Dogs walked twice a day for

5

$10 a week." I called <u>Karen</u> in the morning, and _____ came to meet my

6

dog. Now <u>Karen and Kyle</u> both work for me, and _____ do an excellent job.

7

Practice

Talk with your friends about a way you can earn money next summer. Then on another piece of paper, write a flyer to describe your services and fees. Use subject pronouns when you can.

Tips for Your Own Writing: Revising ....

Do you want to avoid repeating a subject noun over and over again in your writing? If so, replace the noun with a subject pronoun. Remember to let your reader know who or what the pronoun refers to.

 *U*se a pronoun *correctly by making it clear what* it *replaces.*

50 Usage: Object-Pronoun Agreement

*P*ronouns are good stand-ins for nouns. Learn when and how to use pronouns to get the job done!

.... **Did You Know?** ....

A pronoun is a word that can take the place of one or more nouns or other pronouns in a sentence.

> Carl gave the ball to Lou, and Lou dropped the **ball.**
> Carl gave the ball to Lou, and Lou dropped **it.**

Object pronouns follow action verbs and words like *to, for, at, of,* **and** *with.* *Me, you, him, her,* **and** *it* **are used when you are writing about a singular object.**

> Hector gave **me** a piñata from Mexico.
> Did Hector buy one for **you?**

Us, you, **and** *them* **are used when you are talking about a plural object.**

> Mai called Jim and me to ask **us** to the movies.
> We always have a good time with **them.**

....

Show What You Know

Write the correct pronoun in each blank.

1. Jeff was teaching Rita and _____ how to play tennis. (I, me)

2. He showed _____ over and over again how to hold our rackets. (we, us)

3. Rita said it was too awkward for _____. (she, her)

4. Hitting the balls was a problem for _____. (me, I)

5. I spent a lot of time chasing after _____! (them, they)

Score: _____ **Total Possible: 5**

Proofread

There are five mistakes in the use of object pronouns in the paragraph below. Use a proofreading mark to delete each incorrect pronoun and write the correct pronoun above it.

Example: Jessica couldn't find ~~he.~~ (him)

Dad read nursery rhymes to my sister and I when we were young. Each of we had a favorite rhyme. My sister liked "Jack and Jill." Dad must have read it to her 1,000 times! I also liked it, but my favorite one was "Three Little Kittens." That rhyme is about kittens who lost their mittens and couldn't find they. I don't ask Dad to read to I anymore. Now I ask if I can read to he.

Practice

Write a paragraph about something you do with someone in your family. As you write, use object pronouns to avoid repeating the same noun.

_____

_____

_____

_____

_____

Tips for Your Own Writing: Proofreading ....

Remember that object pronouns follow action verbs and words like *to* and *of*. Check that the pronouns you use as objects are *me, it, him, her, us, you,* and *them.*

 Object pronouns can be used in place of nouns used as objects.

51 Usage: Double Negatives

*S*hould you ever use double negatives? No, not never!

························· **Did You Know?** ·························

Sometimes when you write a sentence, you use a negative word like *no*. *None, nothing, never*, and *no one* are also negative words.

> Rob will **never** weed the garden.
> **None** of the yard work was finished.

The word *not* and contractions made with *not* are also negatives.

> I did **not** water the plants.   He **won't** rake the leaves.

Only one negative word is needed in a sentence.

There are two ways to correct a double negative. A positive word can replace a negative word, or the *n't* can be dropped.

> **Incorrect:** There **weren't no** books on the shelf.
> **Correct:** There **weren't any** books on the shelf *or* there **were no** books on the shelf.

Show What You Know

Complete each sentence by writing the correct word in the blank.

1. Most people _____ never get caught in a fire. (will, won't)

2. Never store _____ paint in open cans. (no, any)

3. Don't _____ use gasoline to start a bonfire or grill. (never, ever)

4. Never leave ____ candle or fire unattended. (a, no)

Score: _____   Total Possible: 4

Proofread

There are four double negatives in the note below. Use proofreading marks to delete the double negatives and write the corrections above them.

Example: Sarah ~~doesn't never~~ *doesn't ever* want to go there again.

> Dear Hugh,
>
> I won't never pick flowers in the woods again. There wasn't no warning sign. How was I to know what poison ivy looked like? No one never told me about it. There isn't any way to get rid of it. Nothing won't stop the itching!
>
> Your rash-covered friend,
>
> *Matt*

Practice

Make up a list of good manners. Write sentences using the words *no, never, nothing,* or *none* or sentences with negative contractions.

_____

_____

_____

_____

Tips for Your Own Writing: Proofreading

You always want to avoid having two negatives in one sentence. When you check your writing, if there is more than one, get rid of one.

 Never, no never say, "I don't have no homework!"

Lesson 52 Review: Pronouns and Double Negatives

A. On each blank, write a subject pronoun that could refer to the underlined words.

Christine and I are in the same Explorer Troop, and _____ went on a

1

rafting trip together. Christine asked me if _____ was afraid. This was

2

Christine's first rafting trip, and _____ was a little bit frightened. The

3

guides said that _____ always followed the safety rules and would watch

4

us carefully. The guides were right about the trip down the river. _____

5

was very exciting, and no one got hurt.

Score: _____   Total Possible: 5

B. On each blank, write an object pronoun that refers to the underlined word(s).

Dad asked if my sister and I wanted to go to work with _____. Ariella

1

and I jumped at the chance to see the factory, and so on Friday Dad took

_____ there. As we walked through the assembly line, Dad explained how

2

_____ worked. I watched Dad work on the line, and he showed _____

3   4

how to use a drill to tighten bolts. Just then a whistle blew. All the workers

grabbed their lunches, and we followed _____ to the lunchroom. We ate

5

lunch and then Dad took us home. Ariella and I had a great time at the

factory, and we hope Dad will take _____ there again.

6

Score: _____   Total Possible: 6

C. Write the eleven correct pronouns in the following paragraphs.

One of the three little pigs said to the others, "_____ need to build new
                                                      1(We, Us)

houses." Each of _____ built a new house. _____ used different
           2(they, them)   3(They, Them)

materials to build their houses. Millie Pig told them not to use straw or sticks

to build their houses, but two of _____ didn't listen to _____.
                                  4(they, them)   5(she, her)

When the wolf came, _____ easily blew down the houses that had
                              6(he, him)

been built of straw and sticks. Then the wolf went to the one brick house and

said, "Open up, or _____ will blow your house down." Of course, _____
                    7(I, me)   8(he, him)

couldn't blow it down, and so the wolf slid down the chimney. The pig had a

surprise for _____, though. _____ landed in a pot of boiling water. That
               9(he, him)   10(He, Him)

old wolf jumped out of the pot and ran away. _____ never bothered the
                                                 11(He, Him)

pigs again.

Score: _____   Total Possible: 11

D. Read the paragraph below. Use proper proofreading marks to delete five incorrect bold words and write the correct word above each one.

I don't really **never** like to clean my room. Cleaning isn't **nothing** I would
               1   2

choose to do. Dad said that I didn't have **no** choice. I had to clean my room,
                                          3

or I couldn't invite anyone over to the house. He said that I could have

anyone over to see this mess. Yes, I cleaned my room, and I promised that I
   4

wouldn't **never** leave it in such a mess again.
        5

Score: _____   Total Possible: 5

REVIEW SCORE: _____   REVIEW TOTAL: 27

53 Grammar: Nouns

Imagine a circus in your mind. Can you see the clowns, tigers, and tightrope walkers? Do you smell the popcorn and cotton candy? Nouns are words that make pictures in the reader's mind.

.... Did You Know? ....

A *noun* is a word that tells who or what did the action or was acted upon in the sentence.

The **ringmaster** wore a tall, shiny, black **hat.**

A *common noun* names any person or place.

woman   mountain   school

A *singular noun* names one person, place, or thing and a *plural noun* names more than one.

singular—town   plural—towns

A *proper noun* names a particular person or place. Proper nouns start with capital letters.

Eleanor Roosevelt   Southside School

A *possessive noun* names who or what owns something.

Pedro's basketball   the dog's bone   the actor's role

Show What You Know

Circle the common nouns in the following paragraph. Underline the proper nouns.

Dodoes once lived on the island of Mauritius in the Indian Ocean. Dodoes were very unusual birds. Their wings were very tiny, so dodoes could not fly. A dodo was as big as a large turkey. These birds no longer exist.

Score: _____   Total Possible: 11

110

Practice

Replace the underlined common noun in each sentence with a proper noun. Write the proper noun above the common noun.

Example: Some students in <u>the school</u> are
interested in astronomy.

Lincoln Elementary School *(written above "the school")*

<u>Two girls</u> from our class went on a trip to
1

the planetarium. The planetarium was in <u>the city</u>.
2

<u>One girl</u> asked a question about <u>a planet</u>.
3 *4*

<u>The other girl</u> was reading a book. It was
5

about <u>an astronaut</u>. The astronaut flew on
6

the <u>space shuttle</u>. Returning from space, the shuttle landed in <u>a state</u>.
7 *8*

The astronaut met <u>the President</u>.
9

Revise

Write another noun above each underlined noun to make the paragraph more interesting.

Have you ever visited a pet <u>place</u>? If you have, then you know there are
1

many kinds of <u>things</u> for sale there. In the window, you might see some frisky
2

<u>animals</u>. In hanging cages, you might notice some colorful <u>birds</u>. No doubt
3 *4*

you would see <u>containers</u> filled with <u>animals</u>. In smaller cages, you might see
5 *6*

some <u>animals</u> running around on a wheel.
7

Tips for Your Own Writing: Revising ....

Choose a piece of your own writing. Underline the nouns. Check that you
used the best noun in each position. Using a specific common noun or proper
nouns can add information and interest to your sentences.

*T*he name's the thing! Choosing the best noun for the job will
make your writing more interesting.

111

54 Grammar: Pronouns

*W*hat did the pronoun say to the noun? Anything you can do I can do, too!

·························· **Did You Know?** ·······················

A *pronoun* is a word that takes the place of a noun or nouns. They help you avoid using the same nouns over and over. Pronouns change their spelling according to their use.

John said that **John** was going to ride **John's** bike.

John said that **he** was going to ride **his** bike.

I, *you*, *she*, and *they* are examples of <u>subject pronouns</u>.

Squanto was a member of the Pawtuxet tribe.

He was a member of the Pawtuxet tribe.

Me, *him*, *us*, and *them* are examples of <u>object pronouns</u>.

Squanto showed the **colonists** how to fish.

Squanto showed **them** how to fish.

My, *your*, and *their* are examples of <u>possessive pronouns</u>.

Squanto's friendship was important.

His friendship was important.

Show What You Know

Circle the pronouns in the sentences below.

Have you ever heard of Jane Addams? She wanted to help people living in

poverty. There were no government agencies to help them. Addams established

a settlement house in Chicago. It was a place to receive help and learn new

skills. The settlement house helped many people and made their lives easier.

Score: _____   **Total Possible: 5**

Practice

Write a pronoun in each of the blanks so that the paragraph makes sense.

Four little ducklings pecked _____ way out of _____ eggs. Mother
                               1   **2**

Duck watched excitedly as _____ babies climbed out of the shells. When
                                           3

the time came, Mother Duck waddled out of _____
                                                 4

nest. _____ quacked to her ducklings.
      5

_____ followed Mother Duck as _____
 6   **7**

headed for the pond. One by one the ducklings

followed _____ into the water. _____ all
            8   **9**

swam happily together around the pond.

Revise

Each underlined pronoun in the paragraph below is incorrect. Write the correct pronoun above each underlined word.

Do you like tomatoes? Did <u>we</u> know that at one time almost everyone in
                                   1

the United States thought <u>them</u> were poisonous? People grew tomatoes
                                    2

in <u>them</u> gardens only because <u>his</u> fruit was pretty. There is a story that one
   3   **4**

day a man took some tomatoes to town and offered <u>him</u> to the people
                                           5

who passed by. No one would touch <u>their</u>. So the man ate <u>it</u> all up. <u>She</u>
                               6   **7**   **8**

did not die. The news spread. <u>I</u> helped people change <u>them</u> minds about
                         9   **10**

tomatoes.

Tips for Your Own Writing: Revising ....

When you speak, you can use a lot of pronouns because you can point to
people and things. When you write, make sure your pronouns point to nouns.

*Pronouns make sense when they clearly refer to someone or
something.*

55 Grammar: Verbs

*T*he game is tied. Michael Jordan runs, jumps, shoots, and scores! Bulls win! Bulls win! A verb is the action word in a sentence.

.... Did You Know? ....

A *verb* is a word that shows action or expresses a state of being. Every sentence must have a verb. A verb such as *Go!* can be a one-word sentence.

Jump, shoot, listen, and *read* are action verbs.

Am, are, is, was, were, be, being, and *been* are all forms of the verb *be.* They tell what someone or something is, was, or will be.

A *present tense* verb shows action that happens now.

The farmer **plants** corn in early spring.

A *past tense* verb shows action that happened earlier.

The farmer **planted** beans in that field last year.

A *future tense* verb shows action that will happen.

Next year, the farmer **will plant** barley.

Show What You Know

Underline the ten verbs in the paragraph below. Write *present, past,* or *future* above each verb to tell when the action takes place.

There is an ancient Greek legend about a nine-headed dragon that lived in a lake. The dragon attacked sailing ships. Many people said, "Kill the dragon." Each time one head was cut off, another head grew in its place. Hercules solved the problem. He cut off each head and sealed the neck with fire.

Score: _____   Total Possible: 20

Practice

Write a verb in each blank. You can make the paragraph interesting with the verbs you choose.

A zoo is a fun place to _____. People _____ the way

animals _____. Monkeys _____ up rocks or _____

from tree to tree chasing other monkeys. In the reptile house,

snakes _____ down tree trunks.

Their tongues _____ in and out. The

slow-moving elephants _____ over

to the water in their pen and fill their trunks.

Then they arch their trunks over their

heads and _____ the water all

over their bodies to stay cool.

Revise

Write a more interesting verb above each underlined verb.

Woolly mammoths <u>walked</u> on Earth more than three million years ago.
1
These creatures <u>were</u> about eleven feet tall. They <u>seemed</u> like hairy elephants.
2   3
Mammoths <u>had</u> moss, grass, and twigs. Early humans <u>killed</u> the woolly
4   5
mammoth for food and clothing. The last woolly mammoths <u>ended</u> about ten
6
thousand years ago.

Tips for Your Own Writing: Revising ....

In your own story writing, check that your verbs are in the appropriate tense:
past tense, present tense, or future tense.

 You're really taking some action when you use verbs!

56 Grammar: Adjectives

You've just come home, and you're starving. On the kitchen table is a basket filled with crisp, red apples, golden-yellow bananas, and juicy, ripe peaches. See how adjectives can add flavor to your writing!

Did You Know?

An *adjective* is a word that describes a noun or pronoun. *Crisp, red, golden-yellow, juicy,* and *ripe* describe the fruit in the sentence above.

Adjectives tell a reader *what kind* and *how many.*

Clouds can be **soft**, **fluffy**, **threatening**, or **black**. Adjectives usually come before the nouns they describe but can come after the verb.

crying baby   **six** balloons   **sour** pickle

An adjective is a word that can fit in both these blanks: The _____ tree is very _____.

The **tall** tree is very **tall.**

Show What You Know

Circle the fifteen adjectives in the paragraph below.

On a crisp, cool evening, Donna, a young Alaskan girl, was watching television. A short message flashed across the screen: "Great auroras out tonight." Donna pulled on her warm parka and went outside. Twin pathways of greenish-white light arced across the dark sky. As Donna watched the shining trail, a red border grew along its bottom edge. Suddenly the ball of light exploded, shooting colorful rays in many directions.

Score: _____   **Total Possible: 15**

Practice

Write an adjective on each blank. Two are shown as examples.

On a vacation, a family played a game called "I Spy." Each person described something he or she saw. Then they repeated what everyone else had seen, but they changed the words that described each thing. Here is their game:

"I spy ___blue___ water."

"I spy a _____ whale and ___choppy___ water."

"I spy a _____ dog, a _____ whale, and _____ water."

"I spy some _____ wildflowers, a _____ dog, a _____ whale, and _____ water."

Revise

Write a more descriptive adjective above each of the underlined adjectives in the following paragraph.

When Sara decided to join the band, she had to choose an instrument to play. Would she pick a <u>big</u>₁ trumpet? How about a <u>loud</u>₂ bass drum? Sara always liked the <u>nice</u>₃ sound of the flute. She also liked the <u>low</u>₄, rumbling sound of the tuba. There were so many <u>good</u>₅ instruments that it was hard to decide. What do you think she chose?

Tips for Your Own Writing: Revising ....

Check a story you have written. Make sure you have placed your adjectives before the nouns or after verbs like *be* and *feel*.

Terrific, stupendous, *and* wonderful—*all are adjectives that describe good work.*

57 Grammar: Adverbs

*W*e went to the beginners' band concert. Some students played well, others played enthusiastically, and a few played badly.

.... **Did You Know?** ....

Adverbs can describe verbs. They tell *when, where,* or *how* an action happens.

The concert will start **soon.** (*Soon* tells when.)
The tuba player sits **here.** (*Here* tells where.)
The drummer plays **loudly.** (*Loudly* tells how.)

Adverbs can describe adjectives. They usually answer the question *how or to what degree.*

quite handsome   **too** small   **rather** sweet

My **really** naughty dog chews **very** old slippers.
How naughty is my dog? *Really* naughty. How old are the slippers? *Very* old.

Adverbs can also describe other adverbs.

very quickly   **extremely** slowly   **awfully** quietly

Show What You Know

Circle the adverb that describes the verb in bold type. Then circle the question that the adverb answers.

1. The game **started** early in the afternoon.   How?   When?   Where?

2. The Bombers confidently **took** the field.   How?   When?   Where?

3. The batter **walked** slowly to home plate.   How?   When?   Where?

4. The pitcher **threw** there.   How?   When?   Where?

5. The batter easily **hit** the ball.   How?   When?   Where?

6. The crowd **applauded** loudly.   How?   When?   Where?

Score: _____   Total Possible: 12

Practice

Write adverbs on the blank lines to describe the verbs in each sentence.

Mr. Walsh _____ described the science
  1
experiments to the class. Robbie _____
  2
volunteered to grow crystals. He filled a jar
with water, and _____ added sugar. He
  3
tied a string to a pencil and suspended it in the
water. _____ , he put the jar in the
  4
sunlight. Each morning he _____ checked
  5
the jar. _____ , a few small specks appeared
  6
on the string. Robbie reported _____ that his experiment was working!
  7

Revise

Adverbs add details to your writing. Different adverbs can be used to change the meanings of sentences. Replace the underlined adverbs. Write your adverbs above the underlined ones.

Birthday parties are so much fun. Guests come bringing nicely wrapped
  1
gifts. During the games, everyone cheers happily. They sing strongly as the
  2   3
cake's candles are rapidly lit. The candles shine wonderfully, while everyone
  4   5
waits noiselessly for the wish. Later we talk loudly as the gifts are opened,
  6   7
and each one is lifted slowly out of its box.
  8

Tips for Your Own Writing: Revising ....

Look at a report you have written. Would your report be better if you added
adverbs that tell when, where, and how?

*Surely, you can tell that all adverbs describe verbs, adjectives, or
other adverbs well.*

58 Grammar: Articles

Little words can make a big difference. Good writers pay attention to all details, big and small.

·········· **Did You Know?** ··········

A, an, and *the* are useful words called <u>articles</u>. You can think of them as noun signals. They tell the reader there is a noun coming in the sentence.

A and *an* tell about any person, place, thing, or idea. Use *a* with nouns that start with a consonant.

a ball   **a** jump rope   **a** zebra

Use *an* with nouns that start with a vowel sound.

an egg   **an** oyster   **an** umbrella

The tells about a specific person, place, thing, or idea.

Give me **the** apple, please.

Show What You Know

Underline each word in the sentences below that signals any person, place, thing, or idea. Circle each word that signals a specific person, place, thing, or idea.

We took my brother Jim to college last week. I had never been to a big university before. The campus was as big as a small town. Jim has classes in several different buildings. We visited a science building and the library. The dormitory where Jim lives is a ten-story building. The cafeteria and study rooms are on the first floor. The computer lab is on the fifth floor.

Score: _____   Total Possible: 11

Practice

Choose the article that best completes each sentence below. Write the articles in the blanks.

What if you were on _____ deserted
₁
island and you wanted fruit to eat? You couldn't
buy it at _____ grocery store. You would have
₂
to find it. You will first need to know if _____
₃
fruit is safe to eat. _____ red fruit looks safe.
₄
What about _____ yellow fruit, _____ white fruit, or _____ bunch of
₅   ₆   ₇
green ones? Can you pick between _____ green or _____ yellow piece
₈   ₉
of fruit? How about _____ orange fruit? This should be _____ easy
₁₀   ₁₁
choice.

Revise

Read each underlined article below. If it is not correct, write the correct article above each underlined one.

A animal's tail can come in handy in many ways. An horse can use its tail
₁   ₂
to chase away an insect. An tail of the fish is used to push it through a
₃   ₄   ₅   ₆
water. An monkey hangs by its tail so that its hands are free to find food. An
₇   ₈
beaver smacks its tail on a water when danger is near. A skunk raises its tail
₉   ₁₀
as the warning that it is about to spray.
₁₁

Tips for Your Own Writing: Revising ....

Check your writing to make sure you have used *a* and *an* correctly. *A* is used
when a word begins with a consonant sound, and *an* is used when a word
begins with a vowel sound.

 A *word and* the *word are two very different words, indeed!*

Lesson
59 Review: Parts of Speech

A. Read the paragraph below. Underline sixteen nouns.

Harriet Tubman was born a slave in 1820 in Maryland. She escaped from a plantation in 1849 but had to leave her family behind. Harriet wanted freedom for her people. She helped hide slaves who were on their way to Canada. She was one of the famous conductors on the Underground Railroad. Her bravery helped lead more than 300 people to freedom.

Score: _____   Total Possible: 16

B. Replace the word or words in bold type with a pronoun. Write the pronoun above the bold word.

Kay rides home on the six o'clock train. Every day **Kay** meets Bill on
                                                    1
the train. Kay and Bill give the conductor **Kay's and Bill's** tickets, and **the**
                                                    2
conductor checks **the tickets.** When the train departs, **the train** is almost
3   4   5
full. The conductor talks to Bill and helps **Bill** put **Bill's** briefcase on the shelf.
                                             6   7

Score: _____   Total Possible: 7

C. Underline the verb in each sentence. Write a more vivid verb above each one. You can use a verb from the list below.

unlocked	walked	escaped	will sleep
searched	raced	returned	ate

The zookeeper went over to the monkey's cage. He opened the door to the cage. The monkeys left. The zookeeper looked everywhere for the monkeys. The monkeys ran through the park. They had hot dogs, peanuts, and popcorn. Then they went back to their cage. The monkeys will rest after their exciting day.

Score: _____   Total Possible: 16

122

D. Complete each sentence by filling in the five blank spaces with adjectives.

The baby birds waited patiently in their _____ nest. The nest was

1

safe in a _____ tree. Soon the mother bird returned to feed her

2

_____ babies. The mother bird carried a _____ worm in her

3   4

beak. _____ baby birds and only one worm. What should she do?

5

Score: _____   Total Possible: 5

E. Underline the nine adverbs in the paragraph below.

The sky darkened slowly all afternoon. Finally, it began to snow. The flakes

drifted lazily over the grass and trees. The ground was soon covered with a

soft, white blanket. The wind suddenly shifted, and the storm quickly began.

The wind roared loudly through the tree branches. The snow swiftly piled

against the windows. Within an hour, it was almost a foot deep.

Score: _____   Total Possible: 9

F. Choose the article (*a, an, the*) that best completes each sentence. Write it on the line.

"To live long, live hidden" is the motto of many animals. For some

animals, _____ best defense is to hold completely still so that their predators

1

won't notice them. Some animals are protected by _____ change in color

2

that can make them almost invisible. In polar areas, _____ creature might

3

have fur that turns white to blend in with _____ snow. Spots and stripes can

4

help other animals hide in _____ area with tall grass or leaves.

5

Score: _____   Total Possible: 5

REVIEW SCORE: _____   REVIEW TOTAL: 58

123

60 Grammar: Statements s I

✎ **D**o you know that there are different kinds of sentences? A good writer knows exactly when to use each kind.

·· **Did You Know?** ······························

A sentence can be a statement or a question.

A <u>statement</u> is a sentence that gives information. It ends with a period (.).

Dalmatians are large dogs with black spots.
They do not have spots when they are born.

A <u>question</u> is a sentence that asks for information. It ends with a question mark (?).

How are dalmatian puppies different from adults**?**
What do dalmatians look like**?**

···

Show What You Know

Add a period or a question mark at the end of each of the sentences in the paragraph.

What scared the impala It was a leopard that leaped out of the bush Leopards hunt other animals by sneaking up on them They eat reptiles and small mammals Leopards do not have very many enemies Baboons, lions, and hyenas will attack baby leopards Who is the leopard's greatest enemy It is the people who hunt leopards for their beautiful coats

Score: _____   Total Possible: 8

Practice

Write two sentences that give information.

1. _____

   _____

2. _____

   _____

   _____

Revise

Now, make questions from the statements you wrote above. You can use words like *who*, *what*, *where*, *when*, *why*, or *how* to make questions.

1. _____

   _____

2. _____

   _____

Tips for Your Own Writing: Revising ....

When you are checking your writing, look for sentences that begin with such words as *who*, *what*, *where*, *when*, *why*, and *how*. These words often begin questions. Be sure you placed a question mark at the end of sentences that begin with these words and ask a question.

In sentences that ask, use a question mark; in sentences that tell, use a period.

61 Grammar: Statements and Questions II

✎ *Statements tell and questions ask.*

·········· **Did You Know?** ··········

Some sentences tell facts and others ask questions. Each kind of sentence has its own job to do. Each kind of sentence uses a different end mark.

A sentence that gives information is a statement and ends with a period.

> Most deserts get fewer than ten inches of rain in a year.

A sentence that asks for information is a question and ends with a question mark.

> How much rain do most deserts get in a year?

Show What You Know

Add a period at the end of each sentence that is a statement. Add a question mark to the end of each sentence that asks for information.

Where do the President and his family live The President's home is at

1600 Pennsylvania Avenue Have you ever heard of the White House Gang

They were the six children of President Theodore Roosevelt They had lots of

fun when they lived in the White House They roller-skated in the halls, slid on

trays down the stairs, and walked on stilts in the flower gardens They had

many pets: dogs, cats, rabbits, birds, and a pony Once they brought their

pony upstairs in an elevator What do you think President Roosevelt said when

the elevator door opened Who would have believed there was a pony on the

elevator

Score: _____   Total Possible: 10

Practice

Your home is not as famous as the White House, but there are probably lots of interesting facts about it. Make a list of facts about your home. Use statements in your list.

_____

_____

_____

_____

_____

Revise

Now, pretend that you are giving a friend a tour of your home. Write a conversation that you and your friend might have. Use your list of facts to write questions and statements.

_____

_____

_____

_____

Tips for Your Own Writing: Revising ....

Choose a piece of your own writing. Underline sentences that ask for information. Check to make sure that each underlined sentence ends with a question mark.

Ask me a question, and I will answer in a statement.

127

62 Grammar: Exclamations

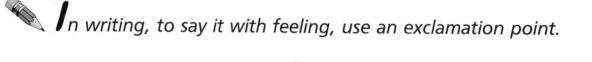

In writing, to say it with feeling, use an exclamation point.

·············· Did You Know? ··············

A sentence that expresses strong feeling is an <u>exclamatory</u> sentence. It ends with an exclamation point.

> It was so hot**!**
> Look at the beautiful sunset**!**
> Be careful**!**

When you are reading, end punctuation marks tell you what tone of voice you would use if you were speaking. In this way, periods, question marks, and exclamation points are signposts for the reader.

Read the sentences aloud. Notice how your voice changes as you read each one.

> I'm hungry!
> Where are we going?
> Nick ate cereal and fruit for breakfast.

Show What You Know

After each sentence, add the correct punctuation.

A little green man was sitting at the table when I got home from school He said that his name was Zornak and that he came from outer space He had eaten all the food in the kitchen Boy, Mom's going to be mad about that I heard steps on the porch Where should I hide him "Hurry, get in the closet" My little brother Eddie came into the room Could I trust him with my secret Here goes nothing I opened the closet door "Eddie, meet Zornak," I said

Score: _____   Total Possible: 12

Practice

Pretend you came home from school and found something unexpected in your house. Write a paragraph that tells about what you found and how you reacted.

_____

_____

_____

_____

_____

_____

Revise

Review your paragraph. Rewrite two sentences to show strong feelings. Be sure to end those sentences with exclamation points.

_____

_____

_____

_____

Tips for Your Own Writing: Revising ....

You use an exclamation point at the end of a sentence to show strong feelings. Using too many exclamation points weakens their meaning. Not everything is exciting. Check your writing. If you have used more than two or three exclamation points, you may want to change some of them to periods.

 When feelings are strong, exclamation points belong!

63 Grammar: Statements, Questions, and Exclamations

"Have I used the correct punctuation?" is an important question to ask.

.... **Did You Know?** ....

Writers use different kinds of sentences.

Most sentences will be statements.

Uncle Jon likes to barbecue.

Some will ask questions.

Does he cook outside often?

A few sentences will express strong feelings, like excitement, anger, surprise, or fear. This kind of sentence ends with an exclamation point (!).

His smoked chicken is out-of-this-world!

Show What You Know

Add correct punctuation to the end of each sentence in the paragraph.

It is a hot, sunny day in southern Florida Do you see an area of swirling clouds off the coast Wind speeds are more than 100 miles per hour Weather reporters name this storm Hurricane Barbara The storm is strong enough to rip trees out of the ground The giant, spinning mass of clouds gains speed over the water The winds shape the clouds into an enormous doughnut Will it move west to the coast, or will it head out to sea Sometimes computers can predict the path of a storm Other times, the hurricane has a mind of its own

Score: _____   Total Possible: 10

Practice

Choose one of the questions from the list below. Write two statements that answer the question.

Should my school require students to wear uniforms?

Is a cat a better pet than a dog?

Do you like the Fourth of July? Why or why not?

1._____

_____

2._____

_____

Revise

Review the sentences you have written. Now change your statements into questions, but not the same questions as those given above. Make sure you use question marks at the end of your questions.

1._____

_____

2._____

_____

Tips for Your Own Writing: Revising ....

Most of the sentences you write will be statements. Check to make sure they end with periods. When you do ask questions, always end the sentences with question marks. To show strong feelings, you can end your sentences with an exclamation point.

When a sentence tells, a period is swell. For a question, it's true that a question mark will do.

131

64 Review: Sentence Types

A. **Use proper proofreading marks to add a period or question mark at the end of each of the ten sentences.**

Koalas are small, furry animals that live in Australia Why did the aborigines call these mammals koalas *Koala* means "one who doesn't drink" How do koalas get the water they need They eat tender eucalyptus leaves that are almost two-thirds water No other animal in the forest eats eucalyptus The koalas spend most of their lives high in the eucalyptus trees Do they ever come down They come down to move to another tree to find more food A koala eats about two pounds of leaves a day

Score: _____   Total Possible: 10

B. **Here is part of a story. The writer forgot to use end marks. Use proper proofreading marks to add periods and question marks to these twelve sentences.**

We have been in the desert for two days The midday sun shimmers on the hot sand We are almost out of water Are my eyes playing tricks on me Sometimes people think they see water in the desert Right over the next dune, I see a cool, blue pool of water surrounded by lush, green trees Is that a camel Is he sitting on a lawn chair sipping a glass of lemonade I run toward the oasis I feel someone tapping on my arm I wake up from my nap at the pool and see my sister She says, "How about a nice, cool drink"

Score: _____   Total Possible: 12

C. Only periods were used in this paragraph. Use proofreading marks to revise three sentences by changing one period to a question mark and two periods to exclamation points.

Imagine living in the age of the dinosaurs. What do you think you would see. The area around you would be filled with unfamiliar plants and trees. You would see some peaceful, plant-eating animals. You might run into some fierce, flesh-eating killers, too. A brachiosaurus was as long as three school buses and as tall as a five-story building. It could have weighed as much as sixteen elephants. Others were as small as a chicken. Ornithopods were little, but they could sprint as fast as a galloping horse.

Score: _____   Total Possible: 3

D. Choose one group of words from Column A and one from Column B to make sentences. Make two statements, one question, and one exclamatory sentence using the correct end marks.

Column A	Column B
We live in a galaxy	a shooting star
How many	around 500,000 million stars in our galaxy
There are	called the Milky Way
Look! I see	stars are in our galaxy

_____

_____

_____

_____

Score: _____   Total Possible: 4

REVIEW SCORE: _____   REVIEW TOTAL: 29

65 Grammar: Understanding Sentences I

*W*riting a sentence is easy if you tell who or what did what.

.... **Did You Know?** ....

A *sentence* tells *who* or *what*, and it tells *what happens.*

My dog Buster   won first prize.
(tells who)   (tells what happened)

. . . .

Show What You Know

Underline the groups of words that are sentences.

1. Harry lives in a cage.

2. A small, chunky hamster.

3. He has a short tail and chubby cheeks.

4. His fur is reddish-brown.

5. The pouches in his cheeks.

6. Sleeps all day.

7. Fruit, grains, and raw vegetables make up Harry's diet.

8. He runs on a little wheel.

9. In his cage.

10. Lots of fun.

Score: _____   **Total Possible: 5**

Practice

Make the sentences below complete. For some sentences, you must add words that tell who or what. For other sentences, you must add words that tell what happened.

1. The girls _____.

2. _____ lived near Boulder, Colorado.

3. Her house _____.

4. _____ wears glasses.

Revise

Read the paragraph. Underline the three incomplete sentences. Add words that tell who, what, or what happened and write the corrected sentences on the lines.

   Our apartment has only two bedrooms. My two little brothers and I. John and Matt are lucky. Get to sleep in bunk beds. I sleep in a bed on the other side of the room. Sometimes, I wish I had my own room. Then my friends and I. Sometimes, I like sharing a room. We all have to clean it even when only I made the mess.

_____

_____

_____

Tips for Your Own Writing: Revising ....

When checking a sentence you have written, ask yourself: Does my sentence tell who, what, or what happened? If your answer is *no,* then you must revise your sentence until you can answer *yes.*

 A *sentence won't work if it's missing parts!*

66 Grammar: Understanding Sentences II

Reading short, choppy sentences can be boring. Once you get your readers started, help them keep rolling. Sometimes putting sentences together can make your writing flow more smoothly.

.... Did You Know? ....

Sometimes two sentences have ideas that are equally important. They can be joined to make one sentence using a comma and the word *and*.

Springfield is the capital of Illinois.
Madison is the capital of Wisconsin.
Springfield is the capital of Illinois, **and** Madison is
the capital of Wisconsin.

If the ideas in two sentences seem opposed to each other, use a comma and the word *but* to join them.

My dog is really ugly.   I love him anyway.
My dog is really ugly, **but** I love him anyway.

If there is a choice in the two sentences, use a comma and the word *or* to join them.

We can visit the aquarium. We can go to the zoo instead.
We can visit the aquarium, **or** we can go to the zoo instead.

Show What You Know

Choose *and*, *or*, or *but* to join each set of sentences. Write the new sentences. Do not forget to add a comma before *and*, *but,* or *or*.

Mary is my older sister. Megan is my younger sister.

1._____

We get along pretty well. Sometimes we fight over using the telephone.

2._____

Score: _____   Total Possible: 2

Practice

Look at the picture. Write two sentences to describe what is happening using *and*, *or*, or *but*.

_____

_____

_____

_____

Revise

Read the following paragraph. Use proofreading marks to add *and*, *but*, or *or* to combine four sentences that you think should go together. Remember to place a comma before *and*, *but*, or *or*.

Example: I like to collect baseball cards. My sister doesn't.

    Do you like to collect sports cards? My sister and I do. I collect baseball cards. My sister collects basketball cards. I keep my cards in a shoe box. My sister organizes all her cards in a photo album. My older brother used to collect baseball cards, too. He doesn't anymore. Maybe he will give his cards to me. Maybe he will sell them. I hope he gives them to me.

Tips for Your Own Writing: Revising ....

Sometimes you may write short sentences that can be combined. Check that you place a comma before the *and*, *but*, or *or* when you combine them. Make sure you use *and* to connect sentences with similar ideas, use *but* to connect sentences with opposing ideas, and use *or* to connect sentences that give choices.

*If combining sentences is what you want to do, a comma and *and*, but*, or *or can always help you.*

67 Grammar: Combining Sentences I

✐ *W*hen two people or things do the same thing, try to tell about it in one sentence when you can.*

························· **Did You Know?** ························

To combine sentences that have some of the words repeated, use the repeated words only once and the word *and* to join the sentences. Remember to change the verb form to agree with the plural subject.

> Maria likes to hike in the mountains.
> Tanya likes to hike in the mountains.
> **Maria and Tanya like** to hike in the mountains.

If you use *I* as part of a combined subject, do not forget to put *I* last.

> **I** am going to summer camp.
> **Keith** is going to summer camp.
> **Keith and I** are going to summer camp.

Show What You Know

Combine each set of sentences below to form one sentence. Use *and* to connect two nouns or pronouns.

1. My grandpa collects stamps. I collect stamps.

_____

2. My sister sometimes gives me stamps. My dad sometimes gives me stamps.

_____

3. Rare stamps are valuable. Stamps with printing errors are valuable.

_____

Score: _____   Total Possible: 3

Practice

On another piece of paper, make a Venn diagram like the one below to show how one of your hobbies and a classmate's hobby are the same.

My Hobby   Classmate's Hobby

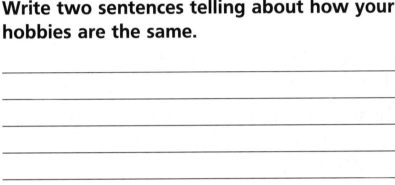

model airplane
my father started
my collection

Both
are
collections.

model car
my grandma started
my collection

Write two sentences telling about how your hobbies are the same.

_____

_____

_____

_____

Revise

Rewrite each pair of sentences below to form one sentence.

1. Peas never stay on your fork. Meatballs never stay on your fork.

_____

2. Lemons will make you pucker. Sour grapes will make you pucker.

_____

Tips for Your Own Writing: Revising ....

Remember that you must change the verb to agree with a combined subject. Also be sure to place the pronoun *I* last if you combine it with another pronoun or a noun as part of a subject.

To combine subjects, the rules are these: subject and verb must agree, and I goes last in order to please.

68 Grammar: Combining Sentences II

If you have one person doing more than one thing, then place the verbs in a string.

.... **Did You Know?** ....

A good writer can combine sentences in several ways. One way is to combine two sentences that have some of the words repeated. Use the repeated words only once, and use *and* or *or* to join the sentences.

Gloria washed the dishes. Gloria dried the dishes.
Gloria washed **and** dried the dishes.

Gloria could dust the furniture. Gloria could vacuum the carpet.
Gloria could dust the furniture **or** vacuum the carpet.

Show What You Know

Combine each pair of sentences below into one sentence that has two verbs, or action words.

1. Helen Keller could not see. Helen Keller could not hear.

_____

2. Helen could read Braille. Helen could write on a special typewriter.

_____

3. She went to high school. She graduated from Radcliffe College.

_____

4. Helen wrote books. Helen received many honors for helping others.

_____

Score: _____   **Total Possible: 4**

Practice

Think about a person who interests you. Write down action words that you might use to tell about the person (wrote, published, invented). Then write two short sentences with compound action verbs about the person.

_____

_____

_____

_____

Revise

Combine each pair of sentences below by using repeated words only once. Use the word *and* to connect the verbs and their objects in the sentences.

1. Frédéric Bartholdi, from France, built a giant metal statue. Frédéric Bartholdi called it the Statue of Liberty.

_____

_____

2. The statue was built so that people can climb up inside. People look out through the crown.

_____

Tips for Your Own Writing: Revising ....

Find a piece of your own writing. Look for two sentences that tell about the same person, place, thing, or idea. If you find any, combine them into one.

One subject and two verbs can be combined to make your sentences more refined.

69 Grammar: Combining Sentences III

If readers you want to win, avoid writing sentences that repeat the same words again and again.

.... **Did You Know?** ....

A good writer can combine sentences in several ways. One way is to use *and* to combine sentences that have some of the words repeated so that the repeated words are used only once.

Kenji likes apples. Kenji likes oranges.

Kenji likes apples **and** oranges.

If more than two things are named, put a comma after each one, and add *and* before the last one.

Veronica has a dog. Veronica has a cat. Veronica has two goldfish.

Veronica has a dog**,** a cat**, and** two goldfish.

Show What You Know

Combine each set of sentences below into one sentence.

1. Our class took a trip to New York City. Our class took a trip to Washington, D.C.

   _____

2. We traveled by plane. We traveled by train. We traveled by bus.

   _____

3. We saw the Empire State Building. We saw the World Trade Center. We saw the Washington Monument.

   _____

Score: _____   Total Possible: 3

Practice

Look at the picture. Write two sentences with compound parts to describe what you see. Keep your sentences short and to the point.

1. _____

   _____

   _____

2. _____

   _____

Revise

Combine the following sets of sentences to avoid repeating words.

1. Elephants eat leaves. Elephants eat grass and fruit.

   _____

2. The African elephant has four toenails on its front feet. The African elephant has three toenails on its back feet.

   _____

3. Today, many African and Asian countries protect the elephants. Today many African and Asian nations protect their habitats.

   _____

Tips for Your Own Writing: Revising ....

When you combine more than two items in a sentence, make sure you place a comma after each item except the last one. Write the word *and* before the last item listed.

One subject and one verb can stand with many words when you use and.

143

70 Grammar: Combining Sentences IV

Sometimes one sentence will do in place of two.

························· **Did You Know?** ·······················

Sometimes you can improve your writing by using one or two words in place of a whole sentence.

Grandma baked muffins. They were delicious.
Grandma baked **delicious** muffins.

You can often combine basic information from several sentences into one sentence.

Grandma has a garden. It is in the backyard. It is big.
Grandma has a **big** garden **in the backyard** *or*
Grandma has a **big, backyard** garden.

Show What You Know

Combine each group of sentences below into one sentence.

1. Rosa is going on a trip. She is going to Dallas. The trip is short.

_____

2. She packs a suitcase. It is brown. It is big.

_____

3. Uncle Larry carries the suitcase to the car. The suitcase is heavy.

_____

4. Doug meets Rosa at the airport. Rosa is Doug's cousin.

_____

Score: _____   **Total Possible: 4**

Practice

Look at the picture and write two sentences with two adjectives connected by *and* to tell what the lucky pirate found.

1._____

_____

_____

2._____

_____

_____

Revise

Combine the following pairs of sentences. Write your sentences on the lines.

1. A sheepdog has long hair. Its shaggy hair covers its eyes.

_____

2. A dachshund's legs are short. Its stumpy legs are powerful.

_____

3. The Chihuahua has bulging eyes. The eyes are very large.

_____

Tips for Your Own Writing: Revising ....

When you are proofreading sentences you have combined, make sure that you have not added adjectives that have the same or similar meanings.

When possible, replace a sentence with a word or two to make your writing more efficient.

71 Grammar: Combining Sentences V

Using phrases in sentences lets you say more—with less!

...... Did You Know? ....

In writing, you can combine short sentences to save space and add variety. Sometimes you can improve your writing by using a phrase in place of a whole sentence.

> My birthday present was a CD player. It was from Mom and Dad.
>
> My birthday present **from Mom and Dad** was a CD player.

Show What You Know

Combine each pair of sentences into one sentence. Use a phrase in place of one sentence.

1. Oscar went sailing. He went with Ramon.

_____

2. They sailed east. They left from the harbor.

_____

3. Oscar had supplies. He stored them beneath the deck.

_____

4. They docked the boat. The dock was past the cove.

_____

5. Oscar and Ramon had a picnic. They sat near some rocks.

_____

Score: _____   Total Possible: 5

Practice

Write a poem by adding nouns, verbs, and other words to the following phrases.

_____ in the house.

_____ by a mouse.

_____ across the floor.

_____ out the door.

Revise

In the paragraph below, combine sentences by using phrases. Write your new sentences on the lines.

Mars is the fourth planet from the sun. Mars is in our solar system. Mars looks red because iron oxide is in the soil. Iron oxide is also in the rocks. Mars is the only planet with ice caps besides Earth. The ice caps are located at the poles.

_____

_____

_____

_____

_____

Tips for Your Own Writing: Revising ....

You can use words like _above, across, before, during, from, in, into, on, over, under,_ and _with_ to begin a phrase when revising your writing.

 "**D**uring the nights and the days" is an example of a phrase.

A. Add the missing words to complete each of the seven sentences.

The animals who live in Animalville lead a different life from most other

animals. In the morning, they _____. _____

_____ have a picnic lunch. Sometimes the baby monkeys _____ .

_____ the trees with balloons and streamers. The baby

tigers _____. _____ make the

other animals laugh. All of the animals _____ .

Score: _____   Total Possible: 7

**B. Combine each pair of sentences below into one compound sentence.
You may want to use *and*, *but*, or *or* to connect the sentences.**

1. Brian and Karen went to the video store. They looked for a movie.

_____

2. Karen wanted to rent *Babe*. Brian had already seen it.

_____

3. Brian decided to get *The Indian in the Cupboard*. Karen liked his choice.

_____

4. They have to return the movie tomorrow. The video store will charge a $2

late fee.

_____

Score: _____   Total Possible: 4

C. Combine the following sentences by making the subjects, verbs, or objects compound.

1. Hidori helped Dad plan a trip. Lee helped Dad plan a trip.

_____

2. In the car, Hidori read. Hidori listened to the radio.

_____

3. They visited a zoo. They visited a planetarium. They visited a museum.

_____

Score: _____   Total Possible: 3

D. Combine each set of sentences into one sentence.

1. Kangaroos are furry mammals. They are unusual.

_____

2. Kangaroos hop on their powerful hind legs. Their legs are long.

_____

Score: _____   Total Possible: 2

E. Combine each pair of sentences into one sentence. Use a phrase in place of a sentence.

1. Bears are big and powerful animals. They are animals with long, thick fur.

_____

2. Bear cubs live with their mother. They stay with her for about one or two years.

_____

Score: _____   Total Possible: 2

REVIEW SCORE: _____   REVIEW TOTAL: 18

149

Writer's Handbook

Getting Started with the Writing Process

Writing is a picture of words.

Writing is like drawing a picture. Follow the steps of the writing process, and you will write a good description.

1. **Select** a topic you know. Look around you for ideas. Draw or write about whatever you see. Let's say you decide to write about your home. Write *home* on your paper and circle it. Draw smaller circles around the bigger one.

2. **Collect** your ideas by closing your eyes and thinking about your home. Write the words you think of in the smaller circles. Don't worry about spelling yet.

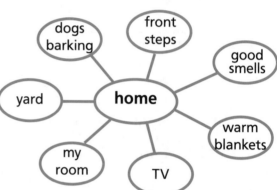

3. **Connect** or group the words in the small circles that go together or tell about the same thing.

4. **Draft** the words you connected by putting them into sentences. Try to describe your home so that someone who reads your description can see it clearly in his or her mind.

5. **Revise,** or change, anything that doesn't fit when you read the description aloud. Ask a friend to help you find mistakes.

6. **Proofread** your final copy aloud. If you find any mistakes, correct them.

Tips for Your Own Writing: ······························

- **Select** a topic that you like and **collect** your ideas.
- **Connect** your ideas that tell about the same thing.
- **Draft** your ideas into sentences.
- **Revise** by making changes and fixing mistakes.
- **Proofread** your paper aloud.

You can "draw" a picture with words.

Writer's Handbook

2 Getting Ideas

Look, listen, read, draw, and imagine! That's the way to find an idea for your writing!

······························ **Did You Know?** ····························

You can get writing ideas from looking, listening, reading, drawing, or imagining. When you are playing, it is easy to decide what to play. Why? You look around and play with whatever you have. You use your imagination.

Your writing ideas come the same way. Look around. Write about what you know or like. Make a list. Circle what you like the most.

For example, try writing the names of three people, things, or animals you know about. Circle the one you know or like the best. The circled word will be the main idea of your piece of writing. Draw five or more lines with smaller circles at the end of them. Next, write something that tells about or describes the word you circled. Does your paper look anything like this?

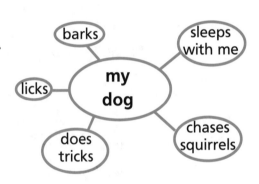

Now you have enough ideas to write a piece. Tell what your writing is about by stating the main idea in the beginning sentence. Then, just write about each idea in the smaller circles. As you write, add ideas as they come to mind.

Tips for Your Own Writing: ··

- Make a list of things that interest you.
- Circle the one that you know about the most.
- Draw circles for five words or phrases that tell about the main idea.
- Write your piece putting your main idea in the first sentence.

Look around you! Write about what you know or would like to know.

3

Writer's Handbook

Writing a Paragraph

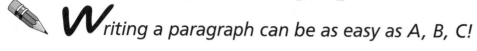

Writing a paragraph can be as easy as A, B, C!

.... **Did You Know?** ....

A paragraph has one main idea. All of the sentences in a paragraph tell about or give clear details about the main idea. They are also organized in a proper order. Read the following paragraph about an airplane ride.

Courtney and I took our first plane ride. We sat in our seats and fastened our seat belts. We thought our airplane ride was exciting.

The sentences are all in the proper order; however, by adding more details you can make it more interesting. Imagine what you might hear and do on an airplane ride. Read the following paragraph to see how more details can make a paragraph more interesting.

Courtney and I nervously prepared for our very first plane ride. The engines were revving up as we sat down and fastened our seat belts. The plane began backing up, and soon we were zooming down the runway. Up in the air and over the clouds we flew. Our ears plugged up and it was hard to hear. All too soon, our ride was over. We thought our ride was about the most exciting thing we'd ever done.

Which paragraph is more interesting? Which one gives you a clearer picture of what the writer was experiencing? The second one, of course! When you write, try to "show," not "tell," your story.

Tips for Your Own Writing: ....

- Make sure each sentence in your paragraph tells about or gives clear details about the main idea.
- Check to make sure that your paragraph "shows" the reader what you are trying to say.

"Show" your writing using details.

Writer's Handbook
Proofreading Checklist

 Proofreading takes a sharp eye!

Did You Know?

Did you ever say to yourself, "I didn't write that!" as you read your paper aloud? Sometimes we don't write what we **think** we are writing. This is why we **proofread,** or check, as part of the writing process.

Here are some things to check for:

1. Read your paper aloud and look for missing or extra words.

2. See if all proper nouns and beginnings of sentences are capitalized.

3. Check for misspelled words.

4. See that each sentence ends with the proper punctuation.

Have you ever been asked to help find something for someone, and you find it right away? In proofreading, you ask a friend to help you find errors you didn't see yourself.

After you have checked your paper for correct spelling, capital letters, and punctuation, it is time to prepare a neat, final draft and proofread it.

See how the proofreading marks from the inside back cover of this book were used to mark the mistakes in the following paragraph.

Last night a small noise woke me up. i quickly sat up in bed. My heart was pounding! What could that be? then I heard another sound. "Meow!" said a little voice. It was just my cat!

Tips for Your Own Writing:

• Read your paper aloud and look for one type of mistake at a time.
• Check to see if any words are missing and if each sentence makes sense.
• Check for capital letters.
• Check for correct spelling and punctuation.

Proofreading helps you make sure you write what you wanted to write!

Writer's Handbook
Description in Stories

 *A*dding descriptive words can make your writing more interesting.

························· **Did You Know?** ·····························

When we tell a story, we use a lot of **vivid** words to make the story seem more real. Words like *soft, bubbly, long, smooth, brown, short, sad,* and *quiet* are some of the words we can use to describe a person, place, or thing. When we use descriptive words, we end up with a much better story.

Below are two ways to describe a room. The words in bold italics are description words. Which set of sentences gives you a better picture?

1. Jonathan has his own room. He likes the way it looks. He picked out his posters.

2. Jonathan has his own room. He likes its *light green* walls and *white* door. It is *small* but *cozy.* On his windows he has *green plaid* curtains. There is a *dark green, furry* rug near his bed. He has a *large, brown* desk. There are *bright* posters of zoo animals on the walls. The posters are Jonathan's favorite part because he picked them out himself.

The use of "sensory" words can help the reader better experience your story. Sensory words you can use in your stories are:

See: *sparkling, spotted, streaked, foggy, green, shining*
Hear: *dripping, sloshing, shrieking, murmuring, crunching*
Smell: *bread baking, vanilla, clean hair, cut grass, gym locker*
Taste: *sour, sugary, lemony, creamy, peppery, sweet*
Touch: *prickly, silky, bumpy, bristly, furry, icy, fuzzy, slick*

Tips for Your Own Writing: ·······························

• Use description to help your reader experience your story.
• Use "sensory" words to help you with the description in your story.

 *A*n absolutely delightful story will tickle your eardrums!

Writer's Handbook

Expository Writing–Writing a Report

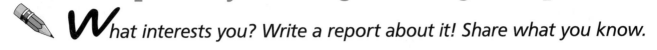

What interests you? Write a report about it! Share what you know.

Did You Know?

Here are the five main steps for writing a good report:

1. Once you have chosen an interesting topic, you can make a **K-W-L** chart.

K	W	L
What I **K**now	What I **W**ant to Know	What I Have **L**earned

List all the things you know about your topic under **K.** Then, under **W,** list all the questions you have about your topic.

2. Your next step is to gather information at the library. As you read, list the most important things you learn about your topic under the **L** on your chart. Then look at your list of questions again. If there are some you have not found answers to, read some more and add notes under **L.** Put your facts in order. This will help you organize your ideas.

3. Next, decide which items under **K** and **L** go together.

4. Now you are ready to write your report. Write all of the important information you remember. After you finish, read your report. Change anything that is in the wrong order or doesn't make sense.

5. Check your work for mistakes in spelling, punctuation, and capital letters. Now write your final copy.

Tips for Your Own Writing:

- Choose a topic you like.
- Make a **K-W-L** chart.
- Read as much as you can about your topic and take notes.
- Use your notes and what you knew before to write about your topic.
- Read your report aloud to yourself and make necessary changes.
- Check your report for mistakes in spelling, punctuation, and capitalization.
- Share your report with another student.

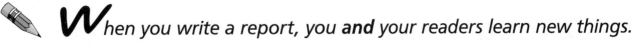

*When you write a report, you **and** your readers learn new things.*

Writer's Handbook

Persuasive Writing

 *My point is . . .*

················· **Did You Know?** ·····················

When you try to talk your parents into letting you stay up later, you are trying to *persuade* them. You want them to **believe** that it is okay. You also want them to **take action** by letting you stay up later.

When planning a persuasive writing, you should first think of all the reasons you have to get the reader to believe or to do what you, the writer, want him or her to do. You can write these reasons in the form of a letter to the person you are trying to convince. Include an introduction that states what you believe or want. Form a conclusion based on your reasons.

Suppose you are trying to convince your mother that you want in-line skates. Write her a letter telling her why you think you need and deserve in-line skates. What can you say that will convince her that you should have them? Also, think of why your mother wouldn't want you to have them and write reasons to convince her otherwise. For instance, if she said that she can't afford them, tell her you will get a job like cleaning yards to earn the money so that you can buy them yourself. You can also give reasons why the in-line skates would be helpful to you and to your family. If you know of any facts or information that would help to convince her, include those in your letter. Every reason or example you give should support your desire to have in-line skates.

Now put all of your reasons together in a way that makes sense. Revise and edit as many times as necessary. Proofread your final copy.

Tips for Your Own Writing:····························

- Think about what you would like.
- Gather and organize your reasons.
- Write an introduction.
- State your reasons.
- Write a conclusion based on your reasons.

With sound reason, you may find a way to get something you have always wanted.

Writer's Handbook

Writing a Friendly Letter

Write a letter and you might receive one!

.... **Did You Know?** ....

Isn't it fun to get a letter in the mail? It makes you feel good. If you want to get a letter, you need to write one. The type of letter you might send to a friend or relative is called a **friendly letter.** You should have a purpose in mind when you write the letter. Maybe you would like to tell your grandparents about an exciting softball game you played in or tell a faraway friend what you have been doing since he or she moved.

Another type of letter you might write is a **thank-you letter.** It should tell what the thank-you letter is for. The following is an example of a thank-you letter:

---

128 Short Street
Huntington, WV 25703
January 20, 2000

Dear Aunt Patty,

   Thank you for sending me five dollars for my birthday. I used it to go to a movie and buy popcorn. I really liked the movie.

Love,
Kaleigh

No matter what your reason for writing a letter, it should be clearly written and include all of the necessary parts: your address, the date, to whom you are writing, the body, a closing, and a signature. (See page 16.) If you are writing a return letter, answer each question that was asked of you.

Tips for Your Own Writing: ....

• Does your letter have all the necessary parts?
• Does the body of the letter give all the necessary information?
• Does your letter have the correct punctuation and capitalization?

Receiving letters makes a person feel special. Writing letters makes the writer feel connected to others.

Writer's Handbook

An Invitation and an Envelope

 An invitation needs to tell what, who, when, and where.

.... **Did You Know?** ....

An invitation can be written in letter form or on cards made especially to be used for invitations. If you are writing an invitation in a letter form, you have to be very careful to include all the necessary information. Those receiving invitations need to know the purpose first. For example, if you are inviting friends to a birthday party, they would need to know that because they would probably want to bring a gift.

Next, you need to let the people know when the activity is taking place. You not only need to tell them the date, but also the day and time. If you want a definite ending time, be sure to include that, also.

Then, add where the activity is taking place. For example, if it is being held outside, people need to dress according to the weather.

If the party is held for someone in particular, such as a birthday party, be sure to give the person's name. Otherwise, just give your name.

Lastly, decide if you want people to let you know whether or not they are coming. Be sure to include the initials R.S.V.P. and your telephone number if you decide you want to know.

When you mail your invitation, the envelope will look like this:

Anita Sang
328 Lagoon St.
Lakeland, FL 32055 } ← *your name and address*

person written to → Amanda Yin
her address → { 254 North Lincoln Street
Lakeland, FL 32056

Tips for Your Own Writing:...............................

• Make sure your invitation includes all of the necessary information.
• Don't forget to include your address on the envelope.

 Invitations usually cover only one subject!

Writer's Handbook
Word Lists

....

IRREGULAR VERBS: Below is a partial list of some common irregular verbs.

PRESENT Today I...	PAST Yesterday I...	PAST PARTICIPLE I have...
am	was	been
begin	began	begun
break	broke	broken
come	came	come
do	did	done
draw	drew	drawn
eat	ate	eaten
give	gave	given
go	went	gone
grow	grew	grown
make	made	made
ride	rode	ridden
run	ran	run
say	said	said
see	saw	seen
sing	sang	sung
sit	sat	sat
take	took	taken
think	thought	thought
wear	wore	worn
write	wrote	written

ADJECTIVES: Below are some adjectives that describe what we experience with our senses.

See	Hear	Smell	Taste	Touch
colorful	crunching	burnt	creamy	bristly
foggy	crying	delicious	peppery	fluffy
red	growling	flowery	sour	prickly
short	laughing	smoky	spicy	silky
six	loving	stinky	sugary	smooth
spotted	purring	sweet	sweet	soft

ADVERBS: Below is a partial list of adverbs that tell how, when, and where.

How	When	Where
loudly	early	back
slowly	finally	behind
too	soon	here
very	suddenly	there

Writer's Handbook

Postal State and Possession Abbreviations

Use these abbreviations on envelopes to be read by postal workers. In other writing, spell out the names of the states.

States

Alabama . . . . .AL
Alaska . . . . .AK
Arizona . . . . .AZ
Arkansas . . . . .AR
California . . . . .CA
Colorado . . . . .CO
Connecticut . . . . .CT
Delaware . . . . .DE
Florida . . . . .FL
Georgia . . . . .GA
Hawaii . . . . .HI
Idaho . . . . .ID
Illinois IL
Indiana . . . . .IN
Iowa . . . . .IA
Kansas . . . . .KS
Kentucky . . . . .KY
Louisiana . . . . .LA
Maine . . . . .ME
Maryland . . . . .MD
Massachusetts . . . . .MA
Michigan . . . . .MI
Minnesota .MN
Mississippi .MS
Missouri . . . . .MO
Montana . . . . .MT
Nebraska . . . . .NE
Nevada . . . . .NV
New Hampshire . . . . .NH

New Jersey .NJ
New Mexico . . . . .NM
New York . . . . .NY
North Carolina . . . . .NC
North Dakota . . . . .ND
Ohio . . . . .OH
Oklahoma .OK
Oregon . . . . .OR
Pennsylvania . . . . .PA
Rhode Island . . . . .RI
South Carolina . . . . .SC
South Dakota . . . . .SD
Tennessee .TN
Texas . . . . .TX
Utah . . . . .UT
Vermont . . . . .VT
Virginia . . . . .VA
Washington . . . . .WA
West Virginia . . . . .WV
Wisconsin .WI
Wyoming . . . . .WY

District of Columbia . . . . .DC

U.S. Possessions

American Samoa . . . . .AS
Guam . . . . .GU
Puerto Rico . . . . .PR
Virgin Islands VI

SPECTRUM

Language Arts

Grade 3
Answer Key

Lesson 1

Lesson 1
Capitalization: Sentences, People, and Pets

At the beginning of a sentence, be sure to capitalize. With proper names, it is also wise.

.... Did You Know? ....

The first word in a sentence is capitalized.
  Basketball is fun to play.
  Where is my basketball?
The word *I* is capitalized.
  Do you think **I** can make a basket from here?
The names of people and pets are capitalized.
  Monica **W**ilson is the coach of our basketball team.
  Carlos is the best player on our team.
  We met **P**atty and **L**isa at the game.
  My cat, **B**oots, likes to play with a ball of yarn.

Show What You Know
Read the sentences below. From each pair of words in parentheses, choose the correct word and circle it.

1. (**Basketball**, basketball) is a fast and exciting sport.
2. In 1891 (james naismith, **James Naismith**) invented the game.
3. Ted and (i, **I**) practice our jump shots after school.
4. My dog, (**Tipper**, tipper), watches us shoot baskets in the backyard.
5. (the, **The**) Chicago Bulls is a championship team.
6. (michael jordan, **Michael Jordan**) was my favorite player in the NBA.

Score: _____   Total Possible: 6

6

Proofread
The paragraph below has six mistakes in capitalization. Draw three lines under each letter that should be capitalized.

Example: today i am nine years old.

  Eight friends came to my birthday party. My brothers, josh and mike, and I planned the party. first we split up into teams and played basketball. Maria made the winning shot for our team. Then we drank gallons of water to cool off. mom knew just what i would want next. she had a big chocolate cake waiting on the kitchen table!

Practice
Write two sentences about what is happening in the picture. Give names to the people and pets.

1. _____ Review the sentences to be sure your child has:
   _____ • capitalized the first word in each sentence.
2. _____ • capitalized the pronoun *I* if used.
   _____ • capitalized the names of people and pets.

Tips for Your Own Writing: Proofreading ....
Choose a piece of your own writing. Look at the first word of every sentence and all of the names of people and pets. Did you capitalize their first letter?

Now you know how to get your reader's attention: Use capital letters!

7

Lesson 2

Lesson 2
Capitalization: Places

From Atlantic to Pacific, capitalizing place-names is terrific.

.... Did You Know? ....

The major words in geographical names are capitalized.

Chicago	**A**rizona	**I**taly
Ohio **R**iver	**M**ount **R**ushmore	**P**acific **O**cean
Lake **H**uron	**A**sia	

  We flew directly from **L**yon, **F**rance, to **M**anchester, **E**ngland.
  The **R**io **G**rande flows from the **S**an **J**uan **M**ountains of **C**olorado to the **G**ulf of **M**exico.

The names of roads, places, and buildings are capitalized.

Fairmont **A**venue	**H**erald **S**quare
Washington **M**onument	**W**hite **H**ouse

  The **S**ears **T**ower is taller than the **E**mpire **S**tate **B**uilding.
  Columbia **H**ospital is on **C**entral **A**venue.

Show What You Know
Write the two words in each sentence that should be capitalized.

1. We're planning to take a trip throughout north america.
   North America
2. My mom works at broadview hospital.
   Broadview Hospital
3. My older brother wants to hike through the grand canyon.
   Grand Canyon

Score: _____   Total Possible: 3

8

Proofread
The paragraph below has ten mistakes in capitalization. Draw three lines under each letter that should be capitalized. Draw a line through each capital letter that should not be capitalized.

Example: Name a famous ~~W~~aterfall in New york.

  Niagara Falls is one of the most beautiful sights in north america. It is on the niagara river about halfway between Lake Ontario and lake erie. The Horseshoe falls on the Canadian side of the ~~R~~iver is 161 feet high. The american Falls is 167 feet high and is in the state of New York. Colored lights brighten the ~~F~~alls at night.

Practice
Write a paragraph describing something you would like to see on a trip anywhere in the world. Use at least four place-names.

_____ Review the paragraphs to be sure your child has:
_____ • capitalized the major words in geographical names.
_____ • capitalized the names of roads, places, and buildings.

Tips for Your Own Writing: Proofreading ....
The next time you address an envelope, check to make sure that you have capitalized all place-names.

Capital means "important." Do you know that Washington, D.C., is the capital of the United States?

9

Lesson 3

Lesson 3 Capitalization: People's Titles

Aunt Sarah and Mr. Lu begin their names and titles with capitals, too.

.... Did You Know? ....

Names showing how you are related to someone are capitalized only if they are used in place of or as part of the relative's name.

Fishing is **G**randpa's favorite hobby.
Every summer, my **g**randpa takes us fishing.
Last year, my **m**om caught a huge fish.
This year, **M**om caught only a cold.

Titles of respect used with names of persons are capitalized.

Dr. Elizabeth Blackwell   **M**rs. Alvarez
President Clinton   **M**r. Peter Tepper

Our class wrote letters to **M**ayor Busby.
Our teacher, **M**s. Whitley, knows the mayor.

Show What You Know

Read each pair of sentences. Underline the sentence that has the correct capitalization.

1. My Uncle has the same name as an American symbol.
   <u>His name is Uncle Sam.</u>

2. *The Cat in the Hat* was written by dr. Seuss.
   <u>He was not really a doctor.</u>

3. In *The Wizard of Oz*, Dorothy called out, "auntie Em."
   <u>At the same time, her aunt worried about her.</u>

4. <u>A main character in *Peter Pan* was Captain Hook.</u>
   He was the mean Captain of a pirate ship.

Score: _____   Total Possible: 4

10

Proofread

The sentences below have seven mistakes in capitalization. Draw three lines under each letter that should be capitalized. Draw a line through each capital letter that should not be capitalized.

Example: His A͟a͟u͟nt is my grandma Andrews.

Every year, Mom, Aunt Tilly, and grandpa Johnson plan a family picnic. Every year, something goes wrong. One year it rained. My U͟u͟ncle said that he didn't know he was coming to a swimming party. u͟ncle Theo always jokes like that. One year, I was stung by three bees. One year, everyone got sunburned.

But m͟om is ready this year. She called the D͟d͟octor to find out the best bee sting medicine. She asked the pharmacist about the best sunscreen. She even is taking umbrellas. My A͟a͟unt is helping, too. grandpa said, "Your mother and aunt will probably remember everything but the food!"

Practice

Write two sentences about a special family celebration. Use family names and titles whenever possible.

1. _____
   Review paragraphs to be sure your child has:
   • capitalized titles of respect used with people's names.
2. _____
   • capitalized names of relatives when used as people's names or as parts of people's names.

Tips for Your Own Writing: Proofreading ....

The next time you write to a relative, make sure you have capitalized all titles of respect when they are used as names or as parts of names.

You're doing a capital job with capital letters!

11

Lesson 4

Lesson 4 Capitalization: Dates and Holidays

"Yes, it's true," I say. "Capitalize days of the week, months, and each holiday!"

.... Did You Know? ....

The names of the days of the week and the months of the year are capitalized.

Monday   **W**ednesday   **S**aturday
April   **J**uly   **O**ctober

Mai goes to the library every **T**uesday afternoon.
The hottest days of the summer are often in **J**uly.

The names of holidays are capitalized.

Labor **D**ay   **T**hanksgiving   **P**residents' **D**ay

Flag **D**ay is celebrated on June 14.
I look forward to **C**olumbus **D**ay every year.

The names of the four seasons of the year are not capitalized.

spring   **s**ummer   **f**all   **w**inter

Show What You Know

Read the sentences below. If the underlined part contains an error in capitalization, circle the word or words that should be capitalized.

We honor Americans who gave their lives for our country on Memorial day. Memorial Day is celebrated on the last monday in may. Some people call this holiday decoration day. Flowers and flags are placed on the graves of military personnel in spring. Many towns have parades on Memorial Day and independence day to honor people who served our country.

Score: _____   Total Possible: 7

12

Proofread

The paragraph below has six mistakes in capitalization. Draw three lines under each letter that should be capitalized. Draw a line through each capital letter that should not be capitalized.

Example: My birthday is in the F͟f͟all on o͟ctober 9.

Groundhog day is an American tradition that supposedly predicts when S͟s͟pring will arrive. According to legend, the groundhog comes out of its burrow on f͟ebruary 2. If the sun is shining, the groundhog sees its shadow. The groundhog will go back to its burrow, and there will be six more weeks of W͟w͟inter. If it's cloudy, the groundhog doesn't see its shadow. The groundhog will stay outside, and S͟s͟pring will arrive soon. An early spring means lots of blooming flowers in april.

Practice

Write two sentences about different holidays. Use a calendar to find out when each holiday occurs.

1. _____
   Review the sentences to be sure your child has:
   • capitalized the names of the days and the months.
2. _____
   • capitalized the names of holidays.
   • not capitalized the names of the seasons of the year.

Tips for Your Own Writing: Proofreading ....

Choose a schedule you have written. Make sure you have capitalized the names of the months, days, and holidays. Remember, do not capitalize the names of the seasons.

Said December to winter, "I get a cap, but you don't!"

13

Lesson 5

Lesson 5 Capitalization: Titles

✎ *Read out loud. Sing out strong. Capitalize titles, and you won't go wrong.*

························· **Did You Know?** ·························

The first word, last word, and other important words in titles are capitalized.

Book: Wayside School Is Falling Down
Movie: Free Willy
Story: "The Fox and the Crow"
Poem: "Books to the Ceiling"
Song: "The Star-Spangled Banner"

Show What You Know

Write each item. Use the rules you know to capitalize each title correctly.

1. "the ransom of red chief"   "The Ransom of Red Chief"
2. james and the giant peach   James and the Giant Peach
3. rebecca of sunnybrook farm   Rebecca of Sunnybrook Farm
4. the wizard of oz   The Wizard of Oz
5. treasure island   Treasure Island
6. home alone   Home Alone
7. "mary had a little lamb"   "Mary Had a Little Lamb"
8. "over the rainbow"   "Over the Rainbow"

Score: _____   Total Possible: 8

14

Proofread

The paragraph below has ten mistakes in capitalization. Draw three lines under each letter that should be capitalized.

Example: One of my favorite books is Annie and the old one.

Not another rainy Saturday—we just couldn't decide what to do! Lisa wanted to go to see the movie rookie of the year. Mark was happy to stay home and read the lion, the witch, and the wardrobe. No one wanted to sit around and recite "The Midnight Ride of Paul Revere." We ended up singing old camp songs like "the bear went over the mountain" and toasting marshmallows in the fireplace!

Practice

Make a list of your favorite songs, books, and movies. Make sure to capitalize the titles correctly. Then share the list with someone.

Review the lists to be sure your child has capitalized the first word, last word, and other important words in the titles.

Tips for Your Own Writing: Proofreading ·············

Choose a piece of your writing that has titles in it. Check to make sure all of the important words have capital letters. If they do not, capitalize them.

✎ *In titles, it's a fact that all important words get capped.*

15

Lesson 6

Lesson 6 Capitalization: Friendly Letters

✎ *Capital letters are the way to go when you open a letter or you close.*

························· **Did You Know?** ·························

The first word in the greeting of a friendly letter is capitalized.

Dear Grandpa,   Hi Leah,   Greetings friends,

The first word in the closing of a friendly letter is capitalized.

Best wishes,   Your friend,
Thanks again,   Sincerely yours,

Show What You Know

Read these greetings and closings for a friendly letter. Then write the correctly capitalized forms.

1. dear Mr. Clark,   Dear Mr. Clark,
2. warmest regards,   Warmest regards,
3. to my favorite cousin,   To my favorite cousin,
4. yours truly,   Yours truly,
5. dearest Aunt Nell,   Dearest Aunt Nell,
6. until next time,   Until next time,
7. very truly yours,   Very truly yours,
8. with love,   With love,

Score: _____   Total Possible: 8

16

Proofread

The friendly letter below has two mistakes in capitalization. Draw three lines under each letter that should be capitalized.

Example: I remembered to add "yours truly," to close my letter.

4 Pinewood Avenue
Alton, Pennsylvania 18106
June 27, 2000

dear Mr. Spinelli,

Thank you for signing my copy of your book *Fourth-Grade Rats*. I do have a question. Next year, I will be in fourth grade. How do I go from being a third-grade angel to a fourth-grade rat? Can I be a fourth-grade good guy?

thank you,

Larry Cosgrove

Practice

On another piece of paper, write a friendly letter to a faraway friend telling him or her about something that happened to you recently.

Review the letters to be sure your child has:
• capitalized the first word in the greeting.
• capitalized the first word in the closing.

Tips for Your Own Writing: Proofreading ·············

Choose a letter that you have written. Check to make sure that you have correctly capitalized the greeting and closing.

✎ *Dear students,*
Without capital letters for the opening and closing, a letter would be wrong.

Your teacher,
Ms. Takes

17

Lesson 7

Lesson 7 Review: Capitalization

A. Draw three lines under the first letter of the nine words that should begin with capital letters.

last Tuesday, I got a new friend. he weighs about two pounds, has four legs, and has brown and white fur. I named him sport. He is a springer spaniel. Former President george bush had the same kind of dog. His dog's name was ranger. Ranger's mom, millie, lived in the White house. Mrs. bush wrote a book that described life through Millie's eyes.

Score: _____ Total Possible: 9

B. The paragraph below has fourteen mistakes in capitalization. Draw three lines under each letter that should be capitalized. Draw a line through each capital letter that should not be capitalized.

The Panama Canal is a shortcut that ships can take between the atlantic Ocean and the pacific ocean. Before the canal was built, ships traveling from new york to san francisco had to sail around south america. In 1904, the united states paid panama $10 million for the rights to build the Canal. Workers from 97 countries from all over the World helped build the canal.

Score: _____ Total Possible: 14

C. Find and draw three lines under the first letter of the six words that should be capitalized.

I looked out into the audience and was glad to see mom, dad, and my brother, Tom. This was my first time playing in the school band, and my knees were shaking. I come from a long line of musicians: grandpa plays the banjo, uncle Bill plays the flute, and aunt Rita is a whiz on the piano. Our director, mr. Lanzt, held up his baton. I took a deep breath and blew into my tuba.

Score: _____ Total Possible: 6

18

D. The paragraph below has ten mistakes in capitalization. Draw three lines under each letter that should be capitalized. Draw a line through each capital letter that should not be capitalized.

December 26 is called boxing day in Britain, Australia, New zealand, and Canada. If december 26 falls on saturday or sunday, the official Celebration is always held on monday. On that day, people give money and gifts to Charities, the poor, and people in Service jobs.

Score: _____ Total Possible: 10

E. Draw three lines under the thirteen letters that should be capitalized in the four titles.

Our class earned $100 to purchase books for our classroom library. We voted to decide which books to buy. The two most popular were the polar express and mirette on the high wire. Nine students picked snow white and the seven dwarfs. Only I voted for talking like the rain.

Score: _____ Total Possible: 13

F. Find the two mistakes in capitalization in the friendly letter below. Draw three lines under each letter that should be capitalized.

456 Kingdom Lane
Happy, Storyland 01234
May 24, 2000

dear Cinderella,

There I was happily eating cheese. Suddenly, I was turned into a horse. I had to pull a huge carriage. Please tell your fairy godmother not to make horses out of mice!

your friend,
Mrs. Mouse

Score: _____ Total Possible: 2

REVIEW SCORE: _____ REVIEW TOTAL: 54

19

Lesson 8

Lesson 8 Punctuation: Periods

A period at the end of a sentence acts like a stop sign.

.... **Did You Know?** ....

A sentence that makes a statement ends with a period.

Kevin let the dog out in the wet backyard.
Blackie tracked mud all over the kitchen floor.

A sentence that makes a request ends with a period.

Please mop the floor before Mom gets home.
Leave the dog in the basement until he is dry.

An initial and an abbreviation of a title end with a period.

Susan B. Anthony   Dr. Martin Luther King, Jr.
Rev. Billy Graham   Ms. Jane Willis
Mr. Lee Seung   Mrs. Margaret Watkins

Show What You Know

Read the sentences below. Add ten periods where they are needed. Circle them so they are easier to see (⊙).

Our village held the dedication for a new park last week. It is named the Franklin D. Roosevelt Park. Rev. John Keats, Dr. Suzanne Reed, and our mayor, Ms. Joan Montoya, each gave a speech. Mr. Edward M. Cameron cut the opening ribbon. Capt. Grooms directed the traffic. Mrs. Mabel Keller and members of her club served refreshments.

Score: _____ Total Possible: 10

20

Proofread

This letter has five mistakes in punctuation. Add periods where they are needed. Circle them so that they are easier to see.

Example: Stop at the end⊙

50 Forest Lane
Fairy Tale Land 43210
June 5, 2000

Dear Mr. and Mrs. Elf,

Thank you for making all the beautiful shoes. My husband, Mr. Shoemaker, and I sold them. The little outfits in the boxes are our way of thanking you. I hope they fit.

Thanks again,
Mrs. Merry M. Shoemaker

Practice

Write the names of your family members. Use initials for their middle names and include abbreviations of their titles of respect, such as Mr. or Mrs.

Review the family names to be sure your child has used a

period after initials and abbreviations of titles.

Tips for Your Own Writing: Proofreading ....

Choose a piece of your own writing. Make sure that each sentence that makes a statement and abbreviations of titles are followed by a period.

Yes, it is official. Use periods at the end of sentences, abbreviations, and initials.

21

Lesson 9

Lesson

9 Punctuation: Abbreviations

✏️ *Make the days and months shorter. Abbreviate them and end with a period.*

························ **Did You Know?**······················

An abbreviation for a day of the week ends with a period.

Monday—**Mon.**	Thursday—**Thurs.**	Saturday—**Sat.**
Tuesday—**Tues.**	Friday—**Fri.**	Sunday—**Sun.**
Wednesday—**Wed.**		

An abbreviation for a month of the year ends with a period. The months of May, June, and July are not abbreviated.

January—**Jan.**	April—**Apr.**	October—**Oct.**
February—**Feb.**	August—**Aug.**	November—**Nov.**
March—**Mar.**	September—**Sept.**	December—**Dec.**

···

Show What You Know

Ramon's soccer schedule has mistakes in punctuation. Add periods where they are needed and circle them. If a day's name or a month's name is not abbreviated, but it could be, write the abbreviation on the line.

Wed⊙ July 14	Friday Aug⊙16	Tuesday Sept⊙3	Mon⊙ October 7	Sat⊙ Nov⊙9	Thurs⊙ Dec⊙19
	Fri.	Tues.	Oct.		
Sunday Jan⊙21	Fri⊙ Feb⊙1	Monday Mar⊙16	Tues⊙ April 15	Saturday May 8	Thursday June 28
Sun.		Mon.	Apr.	Sat.	Thurs.

Score: _____   Total Possible: 21

22

Proofread

These entries from Mama Bear's journal have seven mistakes in punctuation. Use the proper proofreading mark (⊙) to show where periods should be added to the entries.

Example: Feb⊙16. Today is Wed⊙We are having a Valentine's party at school.

Mar⊙14. It snowed all day Sat⊙and Sun⊙night. Papa Bear told Baby Bear to go back to sleep. He said all good baby bears sleep all the way through Nov⊙ Dec⊙ Jan., Feb., and Mar.

Apr. 7. Today is Sat⊙ and Baby Bear woke up. She tried to shake Papa Bear awake. He just grunted and rolled over.

July 21. Last Thurs⊙Papa Bear, Baby Bear, and I went for a walk. When we got home, we found a stranger in our house. Baby Bear cried because her chair was broken.

Practice

On another piece of paper, make a calendar for this month and show the days of the week. Use correct abbreviations. The calendar can be used to keep track of assignments and activities.

Review the calendar to be sure your child has used periods after abbreviations for the days of the week and for the months of the year.

Tips for Your Own Writing: Proofreading ·····················

Choose a piece of your writing in which you have used abbreviations for months and days. Make sure you have added periods after each abbreviation.

✏️ *Shortening the days and months is great, now that you know how to abbreviate.*

23

- -

Lesson 10

Lesson

10 Punctuation: Question Marks and Exclamation Points

✏️ *Mark your questions with question marks. Point out your exclamations with exclamation points.*

···················· **Did You Know?**·······················

A sentence that asks a question ends with a question mark.

Have you seen my umbrella**?**
Do you like strawberries**?**

A sentence that expresses strong feelings ends with an exclamation point.

What a good job you did**!**
Help, I'm going to drop this package**!**

···

Show What You Know

Read the paragraph. Change two periods to question marks. Change one period to an exclamation point.

Do you know how the sandwich was invented**?** It was August 6, 1762, and John Montagu, the Earl of Sandwich, had been playing cards all day and night. Wow, was he hungry**!** He didn't want to leave the game. Do you know what he did**?** He told his servant to put some beef between two pieces of bread. Then he was able to eat while he continued to play cards. Ever since, any combination of filling and bread has been called a sandwich.

Score: _____   Total Possible: 3

24

Proofread

There are three mistakes in the punctuation in the report below. Draw a delete mark through the incorrect punctuation marks. Write the correct ones above them.

Example: Have you ever been to Cedar Point**?**

Have you ever hunted for diamonds**?** Visitors to the Crater of Diamonds State Park in Murfreesboro, Arkansas, do every day. This is the only diamond field in the United States that is open to the public. How can you tell a diamond from an ordinary crystal**?** Experienced treasure seekers know that diamonds have a slick, oily surface that dirt or mud will not stick to. They keep their eyes open for clean crystals. About 1,000 diamonds are found each year. Wow**!**

Practice

Write a paragraph to describe what is happening in the picture. Use question marks and exclamation points in the paragraph.

Review the paragraph to be sure that your child has:

• used question marks at the ends of sentences that ask questions.

• used exclamation points at the ends of sentences that express strong feelings.

Tips for Your Own Writing: Revising ·······················

Choose a piece of your own writing. Rewrite some of the sentences to use question marks and exclamation points.

✏️ *There certainly is a lot to learn about punctuation!*

25

Lesson 11

Lesson

11 Punctuation: End Marks

Follow the sentence trend! With periods, question marks, or exclamation points, sentences should end.

.... Did You Know?......................

A period ends a sentence that is a statement.
  Broccoli is a vegetable that is rich in vitamins A and C.

A question mark ends a sentence that asks a question.
  Do you know anyone who likes broccoli?

An exclamation point ends a sentence that expresses strong feelings.
  I love broccoli!

Show What You Know

Add the correct end marks to each sentence. Circle the periods that you add.

Who invented chewing gum? Gum was first used by Native Americans. They boiled tree sap and let it dry in the sun. This hardened, unflavored sap was called chicle.

William Wrigley, Jr., made chewing gum an American favorite. What is your favorite flavor of gum? My favorite is spearmint gum. It's great. Wow! More than 500 companies make gum today!

Score: _____ Total Possible: 10

26

Proofread

Four of the following sentences have incorrect end punctuation. Draw a delete mark through the incorrect punctuation marks and write the correct ones above them.

Example: Did you know a tomato is a fruit?

Do you know who created Mickey Mouse and Donald Duck? Walt Disney was responsible for making these cartoon characters famous. His company made the first cartoon of Mickey Mouse in 1928. After becoming successful in both films and television, Disney began opening theme parks. Have you ever been to Disneyland or Walt Disney World? They're great vacation spots!

Practice

Write two sentences about the picture. Use periods, question marks, or exclamation points.

1. _____ Review sentences to be sure your child has:

    • used periods to punctuate sentences that make statements.

2. _____ used question marks to punctuate sentences that ask questions.

    • used exclamation points to punctuate sentences that express strong feelings.

Tips for Your Own Writing: Proofreading ....

Choose a piece of your own writing. Carefully check it for correct end marks. Make corrections where necessary.

Yes, positively! I need an explanation. Is this a statement, a question, or an exclamation?

27

Lesson 12

Lesson

12 Punctuation: Sentences I

Sentences are hard to understand when the writer doesn't add end marks where they belong.

.... Did You Know?......................

Sometimes two or more sentences are written as though they were one sentence. The end marks are not placed at the end of each sentence where they belong.
  I am taller than Mary Beth is taller than I.
  Jerry was playing tennis balls were everywhere.

One way to correct such groups of words is to separate them into two sentences with the correct end marks. Make sure to capitalize the first letter of the second sentence.
  I am taller than Mary. Beth is taller than I.
  Jerry was playing tennis. Balls were everywhere.

Show What You Know

Draw lines to show where each sentence should be separated.

Example: I have a best friend | his name is Antonio.

Duke Ellington was a famous composer, pianist, and band leader | his favorite music was jazz. His band played at the Cotton Club in Harlem | that is the section of New York City where Duke Ellington lived. Ellington's band became very popular in the 1930s | the band traveled all over the country. Ellington was one of the founders of big-band jazz | one of his most famous songs is "Mood Indigo."

Score: _____ Total Possible: 4

28

Proofread

Use the proper proofreading marks to show where end marks and capital letters should be used to correct four sentences.

Example: Pigs like to eat birds like to fly.

A terrarium is a tiny earth garden growing in glass. I think plants would be very easy to grow this way. The plants inside the terrarium use the same water over and over again. They are also protected from pollution. The temperature in the terrarium stays the same. Insects cannot feed on the plants. Doesn't this sound like a foolproof way to grow plants? I'm going to give it a try.

Practice

Write a paragraph about what is happening in the picture. Use different kinds of end marks.

_____ Review the paragraph to be sure your child has:

• used end punctuation to mark the end of a complete sentence.

• capitalized the first word of each sentence.

Tips for Your Own Writing: Proofreading ....

Choose a piece of your own writing. Check to make sure that the sentences are punctuated correctly.

Run along to the next lesson to find out more about punctuating sentences!

29

Lesson 13

Lesson
13 Punctuation: Sentences II

Sometimes sentences run on and on and on and they never seem to stop or do they?

.... Did You Know? ....

Sometimes groups of words are put together that belong in two separate sentences. They might be two or more sentences put together without punctuation, or they might be connected with a comma and with the words *and, or,* or *but.*

Incorrect punctuation: This is my pet fish make quiet pets.

Corrected punctuation: This is my pet. Fish make quiet pets.

Incorrect punctuation: These are my cat's kittens that I like to pet and aren't they cute?

Corrected punctuation: These are my cat's kittens that I like to pet. Aren't they cute?

Incorrect punctuation: It is raining, do not let the dog outside.

Corrected punctuation: It is raining. Do not let the dog outside.

Show What You Know

Draw lines to show where each sentence should be separated. Cross out unneeded words such as *and.*

My name is Dumpty Humpty | and I had a brother named Humpty Dumpty.

One day Humpty Dumpty was sitting on a wall | he fell | he had a great fall. I

didn't want Humpty Dumpty to get hurt | but he was hurt | and he was broken.

Score: _____   Total Possible: 8

30

Proofread

Use the proper proofreading marks to show where four end marks and capital letters should be added to create correct sentences. Draw a delete mark through two commas and the word *and* twice where necessary.

Example: I like to go to amusement parks and swimming at a pool is also fun.

Do you think that snakes are creepy, slimy creatures? If so, you have probably never met a snake up close. Snakes are reptiles and they are cold-blooded animals, and cold-blooded animals have body temperatures that change with the temperature of the environment. Snakes keep warm by lying in the sun they cool off by hiding in the shade.

Practice

Snakes are very interesting animals. Use an encyclopedia or another reference book to read about them. Then write a paragraph about snakes. Reread your sentences to check for correct punctuation.

Review the sentences to be sure your child has used end punctuation and capitalization correctly.

Tips for Your Own Writing: Proofreading ....

Choose a piece of your own writing. Read it aloud to check sentences. Correct any sentences that should be separated by using correct end marks and capital letters.

Correct end marks will put an end to incorrect sentences!

31

....

Lesson 14

Lesson
14 Punctuation: Sentence Fragments I

Are sentence fragments pieces of broken sentences?

.... Did You Know? ....

A sentence always has at least two parts. One part tells what happened or what is.

cut the grass   is funny

The other part tells who or what is involved.

She cut the grass.   Miguel is funny.

A group of words that is only part of a sentence is called a *sentence fragment.* A sentence fragment is missing something.

It can be missing the part that tells who or what, or what happened.

Fragment: On the way home.

Sentence: She walked with Alesha on the way home.

Fragment: Rained all day long.

Sentence: We saw a rainbow after it rained all day.

Show What You Know

Read each group of words below. If it is a complete sentence, write *S* on the line. If it is a fragment, write *F* on the line.

1. Yellowstone was the first national park in the world.   S

2. Known for spouting geysers and hot springs.   F

3. The park is located in Wyoming, Idaho, and Montana.   S

4. The park with beautiful scenery.   F

5. You can still see wild bison in Yellowstone.   S

6. See bison in a park.   F

Score: _____   Total Possible: 6

32

Proofread

There are three sentence fragments in the paragraph below. Draw a line through the fragments. Write a complete sentence for each fragment on the lines below.

Example: On our trip. On our trip we saw a huge whale.

Tomorrow we are going to Yellowstone Park. Because "Old Faithful." I hope to see moose, bears, and wolves. Get there. We are going hiking. After hiking for a few hours. We are planning to stay for a week.

Sample answers are given.

1. Because "Old Faithful" is a famous geyser, I want to see it first.

2. I will help put up a tent when we get there.

3. We will need to rest after hiking for a few hours.

Practice

Imagine that you are on this camping trip. Use complete sentences to write a paragraph about your trip.

Review the paragraph to be sure your child has written in complete sentences.

Tips for Your Own Writing: Revising........................

Choose three sentences you have written. Ask a partner to make sure each sentence makes sense by itself. Rewrite any fragments.

A careful writer never leaves any loose pieces!

33

168   Answer Key

Lesson 15

Lesson
15 Punctuation: Sentence Fragments II

✎ *If your sentences are falling apart, they may be fragments.*

.... **Did You Know?**......................

A group of words that is only a part of a sentence is called a *sentence fragment.* Sometimes you can combine a sentence fragment with a sentence to make a complete sentence.

Sentence and fragment: We stayed at the park. Until it started to rain.
Corrected sentence: We stayed at the park until it started to rain.
Fragment and sentence: When Theresa picked us up. We were happy to find dry clothes in the car.
Corrected sentence: When Theresa picked us up, we were happy to find dry clothes in the car.

....

Show What You Know

Combine a sentence fragment from column A with a sentence from column B to make a complete sentence. Write the sentences on the lines below. Put a comma after the fragment from Column A.

A	B
To see Africa's highest mountain	Kibo is the highest peak.
At about 19,000 feet high	You must go to Mount Kilimanjaro.

1. To see Africa's highest mountain, you must go to Mount Kilimanjaro.

2. At about 19,000 feet high, Kibo is the highest peak.

Score: _____   Total Possible: 2

34

Proofread

Combine two sentences with sentence fragments to make complete sentences. Where needed, draw a delete mark through the periods and add commas above them. Draw lines through capital letters that should not be capitalized.

Example: Tom ran after the ball, before it landed in the creek.

Until World War I ended, Most American families did not have a bathtub. Most people did not take a bath every day, Because they did not think it was a healthy thing to do. Early bathtubs were made of wood, metal, or rubber. Modern bathtubs became popular after 1920.

Practice

Add words to make the fragments into complete sentences.

Sample answers are given.

1. When I grow up, I want to be a teacher .

2. I like science , which is my favorite subject at school.

3. Since I want to learn to dance, I signed up for dance classes .

4. Last year when I visited my aunt, we went to a theme park .

Review the sentences to be sure your child has added information to correct the fragments.

Tips for Your Own Writing: Revising.........................

Choose a piece of your own writing. Read it over carefully and look for sentence fragments. Rewrite any fragments to make them into complete sentences.

✎ *Sometimes your mind works faster than your hand. Take the time to write complete sentences!*

35

....

Lesson 16

Lesson
16 Review: End Marks

A. There are nine periods missing in the letter below. Use proofreading marks to show where periods are needed.

7541 Black Oak Ave.
Wolfville, Storyland
June 25, 2000

Dear Mr. and Mrs. Piggy,

My sisters and I are planning a barbecue dinner on July 10, 2000. We have invited everyone from our neighborhood. Ms. Bo Peep, Rev. Wily Fox, and Dr. Mary Lamb will be coming. Dr. Patricia Wolf will begin cooking at 2 o'clock. Please plan on attending. We would love to have you for dinner.

Sincerely,
Big B. Wolf

Score: _____   Total Possible: 9

B. Use proofreading marks to show where 12 periods are needed in the paragraphs.

Have you ever read the poem that tells how many days are in each month? It says that there are 30 days in Sept., Apr., June, and Nov. It then says all the rest, such as Dec., have 31 days except one month. That is Feb., which has 28 days in most years.

There is also a poem that names the days of the week. It begins by saying that Mon. has a child that is fair of face. All other days of the week—Tues., Wed., Thurs., Fri., Sat., and Sun.—are mentioned. These poems can help you remember how many days are in each month and the names of the days of the week.

36

Score: _____   Total Possible: 12

C. Add two periods, four question marks, and two exclamation points where needed.

Did you know that sometimes two birds of the same kind look very different? The male bird is covered with bright, beautiful feathers. Can these bright markings attract female birds? You bet they can! Why does the female bird have dull, drab feathers? Those dull feathers are really a built-in protection. Can enemies see her sitting on her nest of eggs? They absolutely cannot!

Score: _____   Total Possible: 8

D. Delete unnecessary words such as *and.* Use the proper proofreading marks to show three capital letters, and add four end marks to correct sentences.

According to legend, the Olympics began in ancient times, they were started by a Greek man named Hercules. Hercules and his three brothers ran a foot race and Hercules won the race and the Greeks decided to hold more contests to honor Hercules. The Greeks held the contest once every four years, now the summer and winter Olympics take place alternately every two years.

Score: _____   Total Possible: 9

E. Use the proper proofreading marks to correct sentence fragments by taking out unnecessary punctuation. Draw a line through letters that should not be capitalized. Add one missing comma.

1. I think year-round school is a good idea, because it makes better use of the buildings and staff.

2. When kids take computer classes over the summer, they learn new skills.

Score: _____   Total Possible: 5

REVIEW SCORE: _____   REVIEW TOTAL: 43

37

Answer Key **169**

Lesson 17

17 Punctuation: Commas in Series and Introductions

Your audience will give applause if you use commas to show a pause.

.... Did You Know? ....

A comma follows each item in a series except the last one.

New York, Philadelphia, and Chicago have well-known city parks.

A comma follows an introductory word or phrase to separate it from the rest of the sentence.

Yes, Central Park is in New York.

Before the concert, people waited in the park.

A comma is used to show a pause you would make if you were saying the sentence aloud.

We planned a picnic in the park, but we had to cancel it because of the rain.

Show What You Know

Read the report below. Add commas after each word in a series.

There once was a Russian who made beautiful eggs for the czar, or ruler of Russia. Carl Fabergé made eggs that were covered with gold silver and other precious metals. Diamonds pearls and valuable jewels decorated other eggs. There was a surprise in each egg. A small golden carriage a diamond-studded flower basket or a royal crown may be found in a Fabergé egg. Today each egg is worth a great deal of money. Collectors own these special eggs, and they seldom offer the eggs for sale.

Score: _____   Total Possible: 6

38

Proofread

This paragraph on immigrants is missing six commas. Use a caret (^) to add commas where they are needed.

Example: No, I do not like to play soccer.

Between 1880 and 1923, 23 million people came to the United States. Most of these people came from Germany Ireland, Poland and Italy. Many left because there was not enough work in their country. Land in the United States was very cheap and there were many jobs in this country. After arriving in the United States immigrants often settled in areas with other people from their homelands. Areas like Chinatown Little Italy and Greektown sprang up in cities all across the United States.

Practice

On another piece of paper, write a letter to a friend telling about things you would like to do during summer vacation. Use sentences that list things in a series. Use an introductory word like *yes, no,* or *well* to begin one sentence.

Review the letter to be sure your child has:
• used commas after all items in a series except the last one.
• used commas after introductory words or phrases in sentences.

Tips for Your Own Writing: Revising ....

Choose a piece of your own writing. Rewrite it by adding names, action words, or descriptive words in a series. Make sure you use commas to separate the words in a series.

Yes, it is true! Using commas can make your writing clear, understandable, and easy to read.

39

Lesson 18

18 Punctuation: Friendly Letters

Sure, it is an open and closed case, because commas in letters set the pace.

.... Did You Know? ....

A comma is used between the city and state in the heading.

Plano, Texas   Eugene, Oregon   Slidell, Louisiana

A comma is placed between the day and the year in the heading.

April 22, 1996   January 3, 1998   November 10, 2000

A comma is used after the last word in the greeting.

Dear Tony,   My dearest Grandmother,

To my classmates,

A comma is placed after the last word in the closing.

Sincerely,   Your best friend,   Very truly yours,

Show What You Know

Add commas where they are necessary.

1. Mequon, Wisconsin
2. February 14, 1996
3. Dear Uncle George,
4. Yours truly,
5. To my students,
6. With love,
7. Sacramento, California
8. Dear Luis,
9. Grimsley, Tennessee
10. Your best friend,

Score: _____   Total Possible: 10

40

Proofread

Four commas are missing in the friendly letter below. Use the proper proofreading marks to insert the commas where they are needed.

Example: My favorite aunt lives in New Boston, Michigan.

652 Applegate Circle
Lake Zurich, Illinois 60047
May 25, 2000

Dear Grady,

Thanks for taking care of our pets while we were on vacation. The hike through the Grand Canyon was awesome. You can count on me to take care of your dog when you go to hockey camp next month.

Thanks again,

Marietta

Practice

On another piece of paper, write a friendly letter to a friend thanking him or her for a gift or favor you have received. Make sure to use commas correctly in the letter.

Review the letter to be sure your child has:
• used a comma between the city and state in the heading.
• used a comma between the day and the year in the heading.
• used a comma after the last word in the greeting.
• used a comma after the last word in the closing.

Tips for Your Own Writing: Proofreading ....

The next time you write a letter, check to make sure that commas have been used correctly. Add commas where they are needed.

Use commas between the city and state and in a date. Also, use a comma to greet and close.

41

Lesson 19

19 Punctuation: Commas in Dialogue

To separate who said what in a quotation, commas are the punctuation of notation.

.... Did You Know? ....

When you write a conversation between two or more persons, you are writing a dialogue. Use a comma before and after the speaker's words to separate them from the rest of the sentence.

The teacher asked, "What's round on both ends and high in the middle?"
His students answered, "Ohio!"
Dennis said, "I don't like cheese with holes in it."
"Then don't eat the holes, dear," said Grandma.

Show What You Know

Read the jokes below. Add commas to separate the speaker's words from the rest of the sentence.

1. Julie asked ‚"Why are you taking oats to bed with you?"
2. "To feed my night-mare"‚ answered Bill.

3. "Eat your spinach. It puts color into your cheeks"‚ said Aunt Ellen.
4. Cousin Kyle answered‚"Who wants green cheeks?"

5. Carley Cat asked‚"How will I make ends meet?"
6. "Just put your tail into your mouth"‚ advised Melvin Mouse.

7. Paul said‚"Are there any letters in the mailbox?"
8. "No, they're all in the alphabet"‚ replied Pedro.

Score: _____   Total Possible: 8

42

Proofread

Use proofreading marks to add four commas to these sentences.

Example: Pablo asked‚"When are we leaving for the movies?"

Gary asked‚"Do you know why a tulip closes up at night?"

"At night the flower feels cold air and closes its petals"‚ said Gloria Gardenia.

Mr. Greenthumb explained‚"When the warm morning sun arrives, the tulip opens again."

Gloria Gardenia added‚"You know, tulips also close up on cool, rainy days!"

Practice

Study the picture. Write a dialogue for the two girls talking about a movie. Use commas to separate the speaker's words from the rest of the sentence.

Review the dialogue to be sure your child has used commas before or after the speaker's words.

Tips for Your Own Writing: Revising ....

Choose a paragraph from your own writing. Rewrite it as a dialogue using commas to separate the speaker's words from the rest of the sentence.

"Use a comma to separate what was said from who said it," she said.

43

....

Lesson 20

20 Punctuation: Quotation Marks in Dialogue

You can mark my words and yours with quotation marks.

.... Did You Know? ....

A quotation is the exact words that someone says. It always begins and ends with quotation marks. Quotation marks look like this: " ".

Marty asked, "Why do elephants have such big ears?"
"Elephants live in hot climates with few trees and need a way to cool off," said Dr. Bell.

The end marks and commas are placed inside the quotation marks.

Marty continued, "I still don't understand how big ears can help."
"When an elephant flaps its ears, it releases body warmth into the air," explained Dr. Bell.

Show What You Know

Read the dialogue below. Use " and " to show where the quotation marks should be used before and after each speaker's words.

"That was quite a joke Aunt Angela played on us,"said Miguel to Ana.

Ana laughed, "It certainly was. I was kind of afraid to open the envelope when I saw that it said there were rattlesnake eggs in it."

"I was, too, but we should have known better,"said Miguel.

Ana agreed, "Yes, we should have known rattlesnakes don't lay eggs."

"Right. I really jumped, though, when we started to open the envelope and heard the rattling noise,"said Miguel.

Score: _____   Total Possible: 10

44

Proofread

Use proofreading marks to show where four quotation marks are needed.

Example: "No running on deck!"shouted the lifeguard.

"I think we should go to Washington for our vacation,"Scott said.

"The White House is the most beautiful building in the United States,"he announced.

Maura added, "Seeing the cherry blossoms in bloom along the Potomac River is an unforgettable sight."

Practice

Make up a conversation between you and a visitor from another place. Have each speaker try to convince the other that his or her hometown is the best place to live. Use quotation marks to show the exact words of each speaker.

Review the dialogue to be sure your child has:

• used quotation marks to show the beginning and end of the speaker's exact words.

• put end marks and commas inside quotation marks.

Tips for Your Own Writing: Revising ....

Choose two sentences that you have written. Rewrite them using quotations. Use commas to separate the speaker's words from other parts of each sentence.

Remember, when writing people's remarks, use quotation marks!

45

Answer Key **171**

Lesson 21

Lesson

21 Punctuation: Quotation Marks and Commas in Dialogue

When writing conversations, use " " to show quotations.

........................Did You Know?........................

Quotation marks are used when a writer repeats a speaker's words exactly. They are always used in pairs. Quotation marks go right before and right after what the speaker says.

"Mrs. Burns left you a message," said Dad.

If the quotation does not end the sentence, you need to use a comma to mark the end of the speaker's words. Make sure the comma is inside the quotation mark.

"I'm going to give Ling Ling a bath," announced Mai.

If the quotation does not begin the sentence, use a comma to separate the first part of the sentence from the quotation. In these kinds of sentences, place the comma before the first quotation mark.

Uncle Henry said**,** "There's a storm coming."

Show What You Know

Read the paragraph below. Add quotation marks and commas where they are needed. Be sure to place commas and quotation marks in the correct order.

Ms. Carter announced**,**"Today, Mary is going to tell us about something that happened to her."

Mary stood and said**,**"My lamb followed me to school."

"Will he make us laugh and play?"asked Little Boy Blue.

Score: _____   Total Possible: 6

46

Proofread

Use proofreading marks where they are needed. Add three commas and six quotation marks.

Example: "That ride was too short**,**"said Scott.

"I had been asleep about an hour last night when I heard the funniest little sounds**,**" said Monica.

I asked**,**"What did it sound like?"

Monica said, "It was kind of like a bunch of little squeaks."

"What was it?"I demanded.

Monica exclaimed**,**"Winnie had her kittens!"

Practice

Pretend that you are talking to your favorite cartoon character. Write your conversation. Make sure to include both the questions and the answers in quotation marks.

Review the interview to be sure your child has:

• used pairs of quotation marks to set off the speaker's words.

• placed commas inside quotation marks if the quotation did not end the sentence.

Tips for Your Own Writing: Proofreading ....

Find a piece of your own writing. Check to make sure that you have set off the speaker's words by using quotation marks.

When writing someone's words, make sure you keep on track by placing quotation marks at the front and back.

47

Lesson 22

Lesson

22 Punctuation: Quotation Marks in Titles

Use quotation marks with a story's name. For a poem, use them just the same.

........................Did You Know?........................

Use quotation marks around the titles of reports, stories, songs, and poems.

It seems like every year I write a report called "My Best Summer Vacation."
Terrence read his story, "The Day I Met an Amazing Alien," to the class.
I wrote a poem called "The Whispering Pine Tree."

Only use quotation marks when you are writing about the work in a sentence. Do not put quotation marks around the title when it appears on the first page or cover of the work.

Kelly wrote a poem about the weather. She called it "Rain."

Rain
by Kelly Buckley

Show What You Know

Add quotation marks around the titles of stories, reports, songs, and poems in the sentences below.

"Paul Revere's Ride"was written by Henry Wadsworth Longfellow. I called my report"Heroes of the Revolutionary War". Cara's report,"Betsy Ross and the American Flag", was the most interesting."Yankee Doodle"has been a popular American song since the 1700s."The Green Mountain Boys"is a story about soldiers from Vermont who fought for the American colonies.

Score: _____   Total Possible: 10

48

Proofread

Three titles in the paragraph below are missing quotation marks. Use the proper proofreading marks to add them where they are needed.

Example: I called my story"The Mysterious Closet."

Principal Dodds decided to host a public-speaking contest to help the students of Oak Creek School overcome stage fright. Each student picked a favorite story or poem to recite. Tim Weaver recited the poem"Inside Turtle's Shell."Amanda Jones told the Polynesian legend"Why Most Trees and Plants Have Flat Leaves."Ted Redwing told a Native American story called"How the People Sang Up the Mountains."

Practice

Find your favorite poem. Then write a paragraph telling why you like that particular poem. Be sure to tell the name of the poem. Share your writing with a friend.

Review the paragraph to be sure your child has

enclosed the poem title in quotation marks.

Tips for Your Own Writing: Proofreading ....

Find a piece of your own writing that has titles of stories, poems, songs, or reports. Check to make sure that you remembered to use quotation marks.

With stories and poems, both short and long, quotation marks sometimes belong.

49

---

172 Answer Key

Lesson 23

Lesson
23 Punctuation: Underlining in Book Titles

When writing the title of a book, use underlining for the right look.

.... **Did You Know?** ....

Printers put the title of a book in *italics* to set it off from the rest of the sentence. You may be able to use italics when writing with a computer.

Frank L. Baum wrote *The Wonderful Wizard of Oz* in 1900.

When you write the title of a book, you can set it off from the rest of the sentence by underlining it.

The Wonderful Wizard of Oz is still popular with young readers today.

Show What You Know
Read each sentence below. Underline the titles.

1. Little Navajo Bluebird is a book about a girl who refuses to abandon the customs of her people.
2. Harry Allard's book Miss Nelson Is Missing has a surprise ending.
3. Ramona the Pest is one in a series of books that Beverly Cleary wrote about a girl named Ramona.
4. Ragtime Tumpie is an award-winning book by Alan Schroeder.
5. Tacky the Penguin is an animal fantasy by Helen Lester.
6. Toy animals come to life in A. A. Milne's book Winnie the Pooh.
7. Dick King-Smith tells about an unusual kitten in Martin's Mice.
8. The book The Bracelet by Yoshiko Uchida is about a Japanese-American family during World War II.

Score: _____   Total Possible: 8

50

Proofread
Read the letter below. Underline the three titles.

Example: I loved reading Iggie's House.

> 136 Sunnybrook Circle
> Panama Beach, Florida 36890
> October 10, 2000
>
> Dear Aunt Claire,
>
> I was cleaning out my bookshelf and found some books that Lynne might enjoy. When I was her age, Madeline was my favorite book. Since Lynne is in the first grade, she might like Frog and Toad Are Friends. By the end of the year, she'll be ready to tackle Two Good Friends. I hope Lynne enjoys these books as much as I did!
>
> Your niece,
> Michelle

Practice
Make a list of your favorite books. Be sure to underline the titles. Share your list with your friends.

_____
Review the list to be sure your child has

_____
underlined book titles.

_____

_____

Tips for Your Own Writing: Proofreading ....
Find a piece of your own writing that has titles of books in it. Check to make sure that you have underlined them.

Now you know to underline the name of your favorite book.

51

Lesson 24

Lesson
24 Review: Commas, Quotation Marks, and Underlining

A. Use the proper proofreading marks to add ten commas to separate items in a series in the sentences below.

The three largest continents are Asia, Africa, and North America. Africa has many kinds of land, including grassy plains, tropical rain forests, and the world's largest desert. Nigeria, Egypt, and Ethiopia have the greatest populations among African nations. In Africa, there are copper, diamond, and gold mines. Some African farmers grow cassava, cocoa beans, and yams.

Score: _____   Total Possible: 10

B. Four commas are missing in the friendly letter below. Use the proper proofreading marks to insert the commas where they are needed.

> 712 E. 42nd Street
> Albany, New York
> August 20, 2000
>
> Dear Mrs. Kiefer,
>
> Thank you so much for taking our gymnastics team to Atlanta last month. I still can't believe that I saw world-class gymnasts competing in the Olympics. I'm looking forward to working with you and the other team members this year.
>
> Sincerely,
> Kelly McLoughlin

Score: _____   Total Possible: 4

52

C. Read each sentence below. Use proofreading marks to show where three commas should be used to separate the speaker's words from the rest of the sentence.

1. "Please let me stay up late tonight," I begged my parents.
2. "You know that tomorrow is a school day," my mom reminded me.
3. I explained, "This will be my only chance to see the comet."

Score: _____   Total Possible: 3

D. There are eight mistakes in quotation marks and two missing commas in the paragraphs below. If quotation marks or commas are missing, use the proper proofreading marks to add them. If there are quotation marks where they are not needed, delete them.

Heidi asked, "Is Dave at practice again?"

"Yes, he goes to the rink each morning at five and practices for two hours after school each night, Dave's Aunt Helen replied.

Heidi knew Dave never missed a chance to practice his skating. She said, "Well, I guess Dave knows that practice makes perfect!"

Score: _____   Total Possible: 10

E. Use proofreading marks to add six quotation marks around the titles of stories, reports, and poems in the paragraph below.

I called my health class report "The Five Food Groups." My dad thought that "Eating Your Way Around the World" would be a catchy title. Grandpa gave me a poem he wrote about eating called "Down the Hatch."

Score: _____   Total Possible: 6

F. Read the paragraph below. Find and underline the four book titles.

I love to read scary books. Some of my favorite books are It Came from Beneath the Sink, Night of the Living Dummy, and Mostly Monsters. My older brother says The Phantom of the Opera gives him chills.

Score: _____   Total Possible: 4

REVIEW SCORE: _____   REVIEW TOTAL: 37

53

Lesson 25

Lesson 25 Usage: Verbs—Do, Have

*How do you do? I **do** fine, but he **does** fine.*

.... **Did You Know?** ....

Each sentence has two parts: the subject and the verb. The subject tells who or what does or is. The verb tells what the subject does or is. The subject and the verb must work together.

Some verbs have different forms depending on the subject.

Do		Have	
I **do**	we **do**	I **have**	we **have**
you **do**	they **do**	you **have**	they **have**
he, she, it **does**		he, she, it **has**	

He **does** his homework in his room.
He **has** a computer on his desk.
I **do** not own a computer.
We **have** to use the computers at school.

Show What You Know

Underline the incorrect form of the verb in each sentence. Write the correct form above.

1. We <u>has</u> a big old house. *(have)*
2. Dad <u>do</u> the outdoor painting. *(does)*
3. Mom and Heidi <u>does</u> the trim. *(do)*
4. The house <u>have</u> ten windows. *(has)*
5. The windows <u>has</u> many panes. *(have)*
6. I <u>does</u> the mowing. *(do)*
7. My brother <u>do</u> the raking. *(does)*
8. They <u>has</u> a barbecue. *(have)*

Score: _____   Total Possible: 16

54

Proofread

There are five mistakes in using the verbs *do/does* and *has/have* in the paragraph below. Use proofreading marks to delete each incorrect word and write the correct word above it.

Example: He ~~do~~ the dishes after dinner. *(does)*

We all have red hair. My dad and mom ~~does~~ *(do)*, my little brother does, and my two sisters ~~does~~ *(do)*. My mom and brother ~~has~~ *(have)* hair the color of tomatoes. Dad ~~have~~ *(has)* hair the color of carrots. My sisters do, too. People say I'm lucky because I ~~has~~ *(have)* hair that is called "strawberry blond."

Practice

Fill in the name of your community in the blank line of the first sentence in the news story below. Then finish the story. Use *do, does, has,* and *have.*

Today was a big day for the town of _____.

Review the paragraphs to be sure your child has:

* written about their community.

* written sentences in which subjects and verbs agree.

* used *do, does, has,* and *have* correctly.

* written a story that relates to the topic.

Tips for Your Own Writing: Proofreading ....

Next time you write, use the reminder that **he, it, she** (**his**) take *does* and *has.* Other pronouns take *do* and *have.*

The form of do or have depends on who is having or doing. Check on their forms when you're reviewing.

55

....

Lesson 26

Lesson 26 Usage: Verbs—Am, Is, Are, Was, Were

Verbs are sometimes tricky! But you don't need to be a magician to learn how to make subjects and verbs get along.

.... **Did You Know?** ....

The verbs *am, is, are, was,* and *were* are all forms of the verb *be.* The verb *be* does not show action. It tells what someone or something is or is like.

Am, is, and *are* tell what someone or something is now.

I **am** an artist.   He **is** an artist.   You **are** an artist.

Was and *were* tell what someone or something was in the past.

She **was** a swimmer.   You **were** a swimmer.
They **were** all swimmers.   You **were** all swimmers.

Use *am, is,* and *was* with *I, she, he,* and *it.*

I **am**	she **is**	he **is**	it **is**
I **was**	she **was**	he **was**	it **was**

Use *are* and *were* with *we, they,* and *you.*

we **are**	they **are**	we **were**	they **were**
you **are**		you **were**	

Show What You Know

Write *is* or *are* in each blank to correctly complete each sentence below.

My teachers <u>are</u>₁ Mr. Clark and Ms. Juliano. Our school <u>is</u>₂ in Fort Lauderdale, Florida. Luis Mendoza <u>is</u>₃ our class president. There <u>are</u>₄ only 21 students in our class. Most of the students <u>are</u>₅ girls. Mr. Eilert, our principal, <u>is</u>₆ the greatest! The teachers <u>are</u>₇ pretty cool, too!

Score: _____   Total Possible: 7

56

Proofread

There are six mistakes in the use of the verb *be* in the paragraph below. Use proofreading marks to delete each incorrect word and write the correct word above it.

Example: We ~~is~~ on the baseball team. *(are)*

Michael Jordan ~~was~~ *(is)* known as one of the most exciting athletes of the Twentieth Century. He ~~is~~ *(was)* born in Brooklyn, New York, and grew up in Wilmington, North Carolina. When he was a freshman at the University of North Carolina, he made the winning shot in the 1982 NCAA championship game. He ~~were~~ *(was)* a member of both the 1984 and 1992 Olympic basketball teams. He ~~are~~ *(is)* known for his acrobatic dunk shots. Michael ~~are~~ *(is)* a six-foot six-inch former player for the Chicago Bulls. The Bulls ~~was~~ *(were)* the national champions of 1996. Michael ~~was~~ *(is)* now part-owner and president of basketball operations for the Washington Wizards.

Practice

Write a paragraph about yourself and your family. Use the verbs *am, is, are, was,* and *were.*

Review the paragraph to be sure your child has:

* written complete sentences.

* used forms of the verb *be* correctly.

* written about one or two events in their own lives.

Tips for Your Own Writing: Proofreading ....

Begin to keep a journal. Proofread your entries to make sure you used *am, is,* and *are* to show present time and *was* or *were* to show past time.

With the verb be, you are sure to go far if you use was and were when it happened in the past; but in the present, use am, is, and are.

57

174   Answer Key

Lesson 27

Lesson 27 Review: Verbs

A. Write the correct form of the verb on each of the lines below.

1. Larry _does_ thirty sit-ups every day. (does, do)
2. He _does_ them so that he will get stronger. (does, do)
3. He also _has_ a set of weights in his basement. (have, has)
4. Lee and Lance _have_ a treadmill. (have, has)
5. It _has_ adjustable speeds. (have, has)
6. Lee _does_ a workout three times a week. (does, do)
7. Lance _has_ no time for exercise. (have, has)
8. He always says, "I'll _do_ it tomorrow." (does, do)

Score: _____ Total Possible: 8

B. Complete each sentence in the paragraph below by writing a subject noun or pronoun on the line. Make sure your subject works with the underlined verb.

_____1_____ does the cooking at Jeremy's house. _____2_____ has no time to cook anymore. _____3_____ have a big country kitchen. _____4_____ has a microwave oven, refrigerator, and two stoves. _____5_____ have big appetites. _____6_____ have dinner at 6:30 every night. _____7_____ do the dishes.

Accept any appropriate nouns or pronouns.

Score: _____ Total Possible: 7

58

C. Underline the verb in each of the eight sentences below. Then write present or past on the line to tell which tense the verb is.

1. Brian Long <u>is</u> a reporter for the *Newton News*. _present_
2. The *News* <u>is</u> the largest paper in southern Missouri. _present_
3. Brian's first story <u>was</u> about a fire in a factory. _past_
4. Five fire trucks <u>were</u> on the scene. _past_
5. Fifty people <u>were</u> in the factory. _past_
6. Brian <u>was</u> able to report some good news. _past_
7. Firemen <u>were</u> able to control the flames. _past_
8. All of the people <u>were</u> rescued. _past_

Score: _____ Total Possible: 16

D. Each sentence is written to show present time. Use proofreading marks to delete the seven verbs in the sentences below. Add new verbs above each one to show past time.

Mildred Didrikson ~~is~~ (was) an American athlete who was born in Port Arthur, Texas, in 1914. Didrikson ~~is~~ (was) nicknamed "Babe" in honor of Babe Ruth, a famous baseball player.

Babe ~~is~~ (was) a member of the Golden Cyclones basketball team. They ~~are~~ (were) national champions. Babe ~~is~~ (was) a gold-medal track star in the 1932 Olympic Games. People ~~are~~ (were) also proud of Babe's fourteen golf tournament victories. She ~~is~~ (was) the most outstanding woman athlete of the first half of the twentieth century.

Score: _____ Total Possible: 7

REVIEW SCORE: _____ REVIEW TOTAL: 38

59

Lesson 28

Lesson 28 Usage: Verbs—Sang, Ran

✎ *I sang while I ran, although I have never sung and run at the same time before.*

.... Did You Know? ....

Sang and *sung* and *ran* and *run* are pairs of verbs that give some writers trouble.

Sang and *ran* tell about something that happened in the past.

> The Cat Club **sang** in our street until midnight.
> When my angry dad opened the door, they **ran** away.

Sung and *run* also tell about something that happened in the past. They are used with helping words like *have, has, had,* and *could have*. They tell about something that has happened over a period of time or that might have happened.

> The cats **could have sung** all night long.
> They **have run** away, but they will come back.

Show What You Know

Read the paragraph below. Write the correct verb (*ran* or *run*) in each blank.

My mom and I _ran_1 in a marathon race last week. It was the first time we had _run_2 a long race. I could have _run_3 last year, but I didn't think I was strong enough. I _ran_4 the 26 miles in just over six hours. I could have _run_5 faster, but I didn't want to leave Mom behind.

Score: _____ Total Possible: 5

60

Proofread

If the underlined verb is not used correctly, use a proofreading mark to delete it. Then write the correct verb above it. There are six incorrect verbs.

Example: She <u>sang</u> the same song he had ~~sang~~ (sung) yesterday.

The Whittier School Chorus ~~sung~~ (sang)1 for our local cable show yesterday. They had ~~sang~~ (sung)2 many times before with no problem. However, this was the first time they had ~~sang~~ (sung)3 on TV. First, Corey <u>sang</u> his solo. He forgot the words! Mindy and Myra had ~~sang~~ (sung)5 their duet many times before. This time they ~~sung~~ (sang)6 way off-key. The show ended after the chorus ~~sung~~ (sang)7 the same song three times in a row. They never got the words right once!

Practice

Write two sentences using *sang* and *sung* or *ran* and *run*. Use each word once. Read the sentences aloud.

1. _Review the sentences to be sure your child has:_
   - *used sang and sung and ran and run correctly.*
2. _• written in complete sentences._

Tips for Your Own Writing: Revising

The next time you write about something that happened in the past, make sure you use helping words with *sung* or *run*.

✎ *If it happened over a period of time or might have happened, a little help from has or have is needed for sung or run.*

61

Lesson 29

Lesson
29 Usage: Verbs—Wore, Done

✏️ *I wore my favorite jeans today and yesterday. I could have worn them every day this week.*

.... **Did You Know?** ....

Wore and *worn* and *did* and *done* are pairs of verbs that give some writers trouble.

Wore and *did* tell about something that happened in the past.

Worn and *done* tell about something that has happened over a period of time or that might have happened. They are used with helping words like *have, has, had,* and *could have.*

> I **wore** my raincoat to school today.
> I **have worn** my raincoat every day this week.
> I **could have worn** my sweater today.
> I **did** my social studies report on Chief Joseph.
> I **have done** reports before.
> I **could have done** a report on any leader I wanted.

Show What You Know

For each sentence, choose the correct verb in the parentheses and write it on the line.

1. The pioneers ___did___ many new things on the prairie. (did, done)

2. They had never ___done___ some of those things before. (did, done)

3. When their clothes ___wore___ out, they had to make new ones. (wore, worn)

4. Men ___wore___ hunting shirts made from deerskin. (wore, worn)

5. Women wove the fabric to make the dresses they ___wore___. (wore, worn)

Score: _____   Total Possible: 5

62

Proofread

The note below has five mistakes in the use of *wore, worn, did,* and *done.* Use a proofreading mark to delete each incorrect verb and write the correct verb above it.

Example: I ~~done~~ my job quickly. *(did)*

> Dear Jenny,
>   You won't believe what I ~~done~~ *(did)* last month. I tried out for a part in a movie. I have never ~~did~~ *(done)* anything like that before. When I tried out, I ~~worn~~ *(wore)* my sneakers. The movie people asked if I could have run as fast if I had ~~wore~~ *(worn)* dress shoes. Mom told them I could run that fast even if I ~~worn~~ *(wore)* no shoes at all.
>   Your friend,
>   *Enrico*

Practice

Write two sentences about the people in the picture. Use *wore* and *worn* or *did* and *done.* Use helping words with *worn* and *done.*

1. _____
   Review the sentences to be sure your child has:
   • used *wore* or *did* correctly.

2. _____
   • used helping words with *worn* and *done.*
   • written about the people in the picture.

Tips for Your Own Writing: Proofreading ....

Don't forget to use helping words when you use *done* and *worn.*

✏️ *Are you wore/worn out yet?*

63

....

Lesson 30

Lesson
30 Usage: Verbs—Gave, Went

✏️ *Give this lesson a chance to help you with some irregular verbs.*

.... **Did You Know?** ....

Gave and *went* tell about something that happened in the past.

Given and *gone* also tell about something that happened in the past. Anytime you use *given* and *gone,* you need to use a helping word. *Have, has, had, was,* and *were* are helping words.

> Mai **gave** the skates to me.
> Van **had given** Mai the skates.
> They **were given** to Van by his friend.
> Yesterday, we **went** to Sunset Park.
> We **have never gone** there before.
> We **were gone** before dark.

Show What You Know

Write the correct verb in the blank to complete each sentence.

1. We ___went___ to the Memorial Day parade. (went, gone)

2. We have ___gone___ to the parade every year. (went, gone)

3. This year, the mayor ___gave___ some soldiers special medals. (gave, given)

4. They had ___gone___ to fight in Vietnam. (went, gone)

5. Many soldiers were ___given___ medals after the war. (gave, given)

6. Twenty-three soldiers from our village were ___given___ medals. (gave, given)

Score: _____   Total Possible: 6

64

Proofread

The paragraph below has four mistakes in using the verbs *gave, given, went,* and *gone.* Use a proofreading mark to delete each incorrect verb and write the correct one above it.

Example: Last week we ~~gone~~ *(went)* skating at the park.

Every day, Old Mother Hubbard has ~~gave~~ *(given)* her dog a bone. One day, she ~~gone~~ *(went)* to the cupboard to get a bone. To her surprise, there were none, although yesterday she had bought a new package. Because she had no bones, she ~~given~~ *(gave)* the dog some water. The dog then pushed open the pantry door and found the bones he had hidden. He ~~given~~ *(gave)* one to the cat to eat. Then he ate the rest. Now there really were none!

Practice

Write a thank-you note to someone who has given you something or who has done something for you. Use the words *gave, given, went,* and *gone.*

_____
   Review the thank-you note to be sure your child has:
   • used the correct form of the verbs *give* and *go.*

_____
   • punctuated the note correctly.
   • opened the note with a greeting and ended with a complimentary closing.

Tips for Your Own Writing: Proofreading ....

Make sure you use helping words with *given* and *gone* when you write. *Gave* and *went* do not need any help.

✏️ *Have you went/gone all out? Have you gave/given your best effort?*

65

176 Answer Key

Lesson 31

Lesson 31 Usage: Verbs–Ate, Saw

You need a second helping (of helping words, that is!) when you use eaten *or* seen.

.... **Did You Know?** ....

Ate and *saw* tell about something that happened in the past.

Eaten and *seen* also tell about something that happened in the past and are used with a helping word like *have, has, had,* or *would have.* They tell about something that might have happened or that did happen.

The spelling of some verbs changes when they tell about the past and follow a helping word.

I **ate** two oranges and two apples today.
I **should have eaten** some spinach or beans.
I **saw** you eat pizza yesterday.
I **have seen** you pick olives off your pizza.

Show What You Know

Write *ate* or *eaten* on the line to complete each sentence.

We <u>ate</u>₁ very different kinds of food on our trip to Japan. I had <u>eaten</u>₂ fish many times, but it has always been cooked. We <u>ate</u>₃ something called sushi that was made with raw fish. The Japanese have <u>eaten</u>₄ raw fish for centuries. They have always <u>eaten</u>₅ different kinds of seaweed, too. On our last evening in Japan, we <u>ate</u>₆ fish and vegetables fried in batter. I liked that meal the best.

Score: _____ Total Possible: 6

66

Proofread

Use proper proofreading marks to delete four verbs in bold type that are incorrect. Write the correct verb above each one.

Example: We had ~~saw~~ that monument last year. [seen]

We ~~seen~~ [saw]₁ the most spectacular caves at the Carlsbad Caverns in New Mexico. I had never ~~saw~~ [seen]₂ such large underground rooms. We saw formations called stalagmites that looked like icicles growing up from the cavern's floor. We ~~seen~~ [saw]₃ some that had grown to be more than sixty feet tall. If we had walked farther into the cavern, we could have ~~saw~~ [seen]₄ a rock formation called the Bashful Elephant.

Practice

Write a paragraph about the best meal that you have ever eaten. Write about how the food looked and tasted. Use the words *ate, eaten, saw,* and *seen.*

Review the paragraph to be sure your child has:

• used the words *ate* and *eaten* correctly.

• used the words *saw* and *seen* correctly.

• punctuated the sentences correctly.

• written about a meal.

Tips for Your Own Writing: Proofreading ....

When you use the words *eaten* and *seen* in your writing, make sure you always give them help by using words such as *have, has,* and *had.*

If you have saw the mistake in this sentence, you understand this lesson.

67

....

Lesson 32

Lesson 32 Review: Verbs

A. Write the correct verb in the blanks from each pair of verbs in parentheses.

(sang, sung)

What was I going to do? Baby Lauren wouldn't go to sleep. I <u>sang</u>₁ every lullaby I knew. Then Grandma <u>sang</u>₂ a song from a commercial on TV. Lauren went right to sleep. Grandma laughed, "I have <u>sung</u>₃ that song many times. I know it works. Every time Grandpa hears it, he dozes right off!"

(ran, run)

The gust of wind caught Tito's kite and blew it high into the sky. Tito <u>ran</u>₄ over the hill, clenching his kite string in his hand. The kite continued to drift toward the pond. When Tito had <u>run</u>₅ as far as he could, he stopped. If he <u>ran</u>₆ any farther, he would be knee-deep in water. He slowly let go of the kite.

Score: _____ Total Possible: 6

B. Write the correct verb in each blank.

1. Mrs. Cain <u>did</u> a good job making costumes for the play. (did, done)

2. Mia <u>wore</u> a dress that looked just like a real queen's gown. (wore, worn)

3. Her red shoes had been <u>worn</u> in last year's play. (wore, worn)

4. She also <u>wore</u> a cape Mrs. Cain made from old curtains. (wore, worn)

5. Mrs. Cain had <u>done</u> a great job painting the scenery. (did, done)

Score: _____ Total Possible: 5

68

C. Write the correct verb—*gave, given, went,* or *gone*—in each blank. Then write four sentences of your own using each of the verbs.

1. Grandma and Grandpa <u>went</u> on a trip to Switzerland.

2. They had <u>gone</u> to Ireland the year before.

3. They <u>gave</u> each grandchild a cuckoo clock.

4. No one had ever <u>given</u> me such an unusual clock before.

1. _Sentences should use each verb form correctly._
2. _____
3. _____
4. _____

Score: _____ Total Possible: 8

D. Choose a verb from those listed below to complete each sentence. Write the correct word in each blank.

ate	eaten	saw	seen

I thought I had <u>seen</u>₁ everything until I went to the Plainfield Pie Eating Contest! I <u>saw</u>₂ some people eating apple, cherry, blueberry, and peach pies. Others <u>ate</u>₃ strawberry and banana cream pies. Some people <u>ate</u>₄ more than one. A few people had <u>eaten</u>₅ pie since six in the morning. I <u>ate</u>₆ a slice of chocolate cream pie. Then I saw something called shoofly pie. I would have <u>eaten</u>₇ a piece, but I usually don't eat bugs!

Score: _____ Total Possible: 7

REVIEW SCORE: _____ REVIEW TOTAL: 26

69

Lesson 33

Lesson
33 Usage: Adjectives

✐ *Use bigger for two and biggest for more than two when comparing is what you want to do.*

.... **Did You Know?** ....

Adjectives are words that describe nouns.

The ending *-er* is added to most adjectives that compare two people, places, or things. The ending *-est* is added to most adjectives to compare more than two people, places, or things.

> A coyote can run **faster** than a bear.
> The cheetah is the **fastest** animal of all.

If the adjective ends with an *e*, drop the *e* before adding the *-er* or *-est* ending.

> large   larg**er**   larg**est**

If the adjective ends with a single vowel and a consonant, double the consonant and add the *-er* or *-est* ending.

> big   big**ger**   big**gest**

If the adjective ends with a consonant and *y*, change the *y* to *i* before adding *-er* or *-est*.

> tiny   tin**ier**   tin**iest**

Some long adjectives use *more* and *most*.

> beautiful   **more** beautiful   **most** beautiful

....

Show What You Know
Write the correct adjective on each line.

1. We just had the ___hottest___ summer in history. (hotter, hottest)

2. Dad was ___happier___ about the weather than we were. (happier, happiest)

3. His roses were ___more beautiful___ than ever. (more beautiful, most beautiful)

Score: _____   Total Possible: 3

70

Proofread
The paragraph below has five mistakes in adjectives that compare. Use a proofreading mark to delete each incorrect adjective and write the correct one above it.

Example: We picked the ~~bigger~~ biggest apples in the orchard.

The ~~larger~~ largest trees in the world live in the Sequoia National Park in California. The park was created to protect these ~~more~~ most amazing trees. Unlike other trees, the giant sequoia's trunk does not get thinner at the top. Some trees are ~~widest~~ wider than a city street. The ~~taller~~ tallest tree in the park is 310 feet high. The tree called General Sherman is the overall ~~bigger~~ biggest tree in the world. It weighs 6,000 tons and is still growing!

Practice
Write three sentences about the picture comparing the objects that you see. Use adjectives like *busy, loud, quiet, small, slow,* and *happy.*

Review the sentences to be sure your child has:

• used adjectives in comparisons.

• written complete sentences with correct end punctuation.

• used the correct endings for adjectives that compare.

• written sentences related to the picture.

Tips for Your Own Writing: Proofreading
When you are writing comparisons, think of the words *better* and *best*. The *-er* in *better* stands for two and the *-est* in *best* stands for more than two.

✐ *You couldn't do better if you did your best job on this lesson.*

71

....

Lesson 34

Lesson
34 Usage: Homophones—Hear/Here, To/Too/Two

✐ *Hear! Hear! Here are two homophones that sound the same but are confusing, too—hear/here and to/too/two.*

.... **Did You Know?** ....

Words that sound alike but are spelled differently and have different meanings are called homophones.

Hear and *here* are homophones. *Hear* means "to listen to something." *Here* means "at" or "in this place." A good way to remember the difference is that *hear* has an "ear" in it.

> Can you **hear** it ring?
> I am going to put the telephone over **here**.

Another example is *to, too,* and *two*. *To* means "toward." *Too* means "also" or "more than enough." *Two* is the number between one and three.

> Maggie and Theresa went **to** the movies and ate **two** bags of popcorn. They drank lemonade, **too**.

....

Show What You Know
Write the correct homophone in each sentence below.

1. "I'm going ___to___ the tennis court," Meg announced. (too, to, two)

2. Her younger sister, Peg, asked, "May I go, ___too___?" (too, to, two)

3. Meg said, "Sure, tennis is a game for ___two___ people." (too, to, two)

4. Meg added, "___Here___, you may use my old racket." (Here, Hear)

5. Peg asked, "Do you ___hear___ Mom calling us?" (hear, here)

72

Score: _____   Total Possible: 5

Proofread
Use proper proofreading marks to delete nine incorrect homophones in the story below. Write the correct homophone above each one.

Example: She didn't ~~here~~ hear what you said.

Nick and Alex found an old pirate map and decided ~~two~~ to find the buried treasure. Nick read, "Follow the shoreline ~~two~~ to [1] the entrance ~~too~~ to [2] the cave." The ~~to~~ two [4] boys found and entered the cave. "Do you ~~here~~ hear [5] something?" asked Nick.

Alex called **to** Nick, "I think it's coming from over ~~heat~~ here [6]." ~~To~~ Two [8] furry bats hung from the ceiling above a battered, old chest. Alex took one look at the bats and said, "I'm out of ~~heat~~ here [9]!"

Nick quickly turned and said, "Me, ~~twe!~~ too [10]!"

Practice
Write two sentences about what the people in the picture might be saying to each other. Use the words *to, too, two, here,* and *hear.*

Review the sentences to be sure your child has:

• used the homophones listed above correctly.

• capitalized the first word in each sentence.

• punctuated each sentence correctly.

Tips for Your Own Writing: Proofreading
Remember that *two* is a number for one more than one, and *too* is *too* much, or more than enough.

✐ *This lesson teaches about to/too/two homophones in which you cannot here/hear a difference in meaning.*

73

Lesson 35

Lesson
35 Usage: Homophones–Its/It's

When you shorten it is, you write it's, but when it owns something, you write its.

.... **Did You Know?** ....

How to write these two little words, *its* and *it's*, commonly confuses writers.

Its is a word that shows ownership. *Its* is a personal pronoun that shows possession.

The school lost **its** power during the storm.

It's is a contraction. The apostrophe reminds you that *it's* stands for the two words *it is.*

It's going to be out for the rest of the day.

....

Show What You Know

Write *its* or *it's* to correctly complete each sentence below.

1. Listen, __it's__ the sound of a kitten crying.

2. I hope __it's__ not lost.

3. The kitten can't find __its__ way home.

4. What is __its__ name?

5. I don't know because __it's__ not on __its__ collar.

6. Who is __its__ owner?

7. Let's look on __its__ collar to find out.

8. __It's__ kind to help a lost animal.

Score: _____   Total Possible: 9

74

Proofread

Use proofreading marks to delete each homophone in bold type that is incorrect. Write the correct word above it. There are four errors.

Example: ~~Its~~ _It's_ time to go home.

The desert can be hot and dry. A desert plant has to adapt to ~~it's~~ _its_ climate.
[1]
A cactus has thousands of widespread roots under the ground's surface.
When it rains, **its** roots quickly absorb water. After a rainstorm, ~~its~~ _it's_ possible
[2]   [3]
for a cactus to be filled with water! ~~It's~~ _Its_ thick, tough skin helps to prevent the
[4]
water from evaporating. A cactus has small, hairy pads on ~~it's~~ _its_ stem called
[5]
areoles. Thorns, flowers, or new branches grow from these.

Practice

Write a paragraph describing a plant that grows where you live. Use *it's* and *its* each at least once.

_____ Review the paragraph to be sure your child has: _____

• used *its* and *it's* correctly.

• written complete sentences.

• provided accurate information about their chosen plant.

Tips for Your Own Writing: Proofreading ....

Review a paper you have written describing something. Check to see that if you wrote about ownership, you used *its*, and if you used a contraction for *it is*, you wrote *it's*.

If its shows what is owned, then it stands alone—no apostrophe. If it's is a contraction, then an apostrophe is part of the action.

75

Lesson 36

Lesson
36 Review: Adjectives and Homophones

A. Write the correct adjective in the blank to complete each sentence.

1. Daryl is the _____tallest_____ of the three Robey brothers. (taller, tallest)

2. He is also _____more unusual_____ than his brothers. (more unusual, most unusual)

3. Daryl has _____longer_____ hair than both his brothers. (longer, longest)

4. This week it is the _____brightest_____ shade of purple you can imagine.
   (brighter, brightest)

5. Last week, it was an even _____uglier_____ color. (uglier, ugliest)

6. Daryl has the _____strangest_____ hair of anyone I know. (stranger, strangest)

7. He's also the _____friendliest_____ guy in the world! (friendlier, friendliest)

Score: _____   Total Possible: 7

B. The paragraph below has six mistakes in adjectives that compare. Use a proofreading mark to delete each incorrect adjective and write the correct one above it.

Alaskan brown bears and grizzly bears are the ~~larger~~ _largest_ bears in the world.
They are easily angered but usually will not attack unless they are threatened.
The American black bear is the most ~~commonest~~ _common_ species. These bears are fast
runners and agile climbers. Asiatic black bears are ~~smallest~~ _smaller_ than American
black bears. They are also ~~fiercest~~ _fiercer_ than most other kinds of bears. Sun bears
are the ~~most small~~ _smallest_ kind of bear. Their claws are more curved and have
~~sharpest~~ _sharper_ points than those of any other kind of bear. Bears spend the day
sleeping and the night hunting for food.

Score: _____   Total Possible: 6

76

C. Write the correct homophone to complete each sentence.

1. Dad said I could invite _____two_____ friends to the ball game. (to, too, two)

2. I asked Jonah and Julie _____to_____ come with us. (to, too, two)

3. We all wanted to _____hear_____ the announcer sing. (hear, here)

4. He always sings, "Take Me Out _____to_____ the Ball Game." (to, too, two)

5. Driving to the game, traffic was backed up _____two_____ miles. (to, too, two)

6. Finally, Dad reached a parking lot and said, "We'll park _____here_____." (hear, here)

7. Many other cars pulled into the lot, _____too_____. (to, too, two)

Score: _____   Total Possible: 7

D. Write *its* or *it's* on each line to complete the sentences below.

What swims slowly through the warm tropical water? _____its_____ head is
[1]
like a horse's and _____its_____ tail is like a monkey's. _____It's_____ a sea horse! It
[2]   [3]
carries _____its_____ baby sea horses in a pouch until they're ready to be born.
[4]
But _____it's_____ not the mother that carries the babies. _____It's_____ the father! A
[5]   [6]
father sea horse carries hundreds of babies in _____its_____ pouch. Baby sea
[7]
horses can look after themselves as soon as they are born.

Score: _____   Total Possible: 7

REVIEW SCORE: _____   REVIEW TOTAL: 27

77

Answer Key 179

Lesson 37

Lesson 37 Usage: Regular Plurals

There are plural (more than one) ways to make a word plural!

.... **Did You Know?** ....

A noun that stands for one person, place, or thing is *singular*.

The clown sharpened the huge **pencil**.

A noun that stands for more than one person, place, or thing is *plural*.

The clown sharpened four huge **pencils**.

Add *-s* to the ends of most nouns to form the plural.

Add *-es* to nouns ending in *-s, ss, x, ch,* or *sh.*

class–class**es**   peach–peach**es**
brush–brush**es**   box–box**es**

Change the *y* to *i* and add *-es* to nouns that end in a consonant and *y*.

sky–sk**ies**   story–stor**ies**

Show What You Know

Write a plural noun above for each singular noun that is underlined.

The <u>beach</u> [beaches] on this island are sandy. Sometimes the <u>wave</u> [waves] crash against
                    1   2
the pier. Many <u>family</u> [families] come here to play in the sun. My family comes here on
              3
<u>Sunday</u> [Sundays] during the summer. Terri likes to search for <u>shell</u> [shells]. She has <u>box</u> [boxes] filled
    4   5   6
with them. Angela builds <u>sand castle</u> [sand castles]. Dad spends his whole time taking
                        7
<u>photo</u> [photos] of us.
    8

Score: _____   Total Possible: 8

78

Proofread

There are six incorrect plurals in the paragraph below. Use a proofreading mark to delete each underlined word that is incorrect and write the correct plural above it.

Example: He is listening to ~~storys~~ [stories] on the radio.

Jeremy has two ~~gardenes~~ [gardens] in his yard. In one garden, he grows ~~petuniaes~~ [petunias]
                    1
and <u>daisies</u>. In the other, he grows ~~carrotes~~ [carrots] and ~~beanes~~ [beans]. There are raspberry
                                    3   4
~~bushs~~ [bushes] along the edge of the garden. Yesterday, Jeremy picked ~~bunchs~~ [bunches] of
    6   7
fresh, green spinach for dinner.

Practice

Write a paragraph describing what is happening in the picture. Use plural nouns.

Review the paragraph to be sure your child has:

• written a paragraph about an event in the picture.

• correctly added -s or -es to nouns to form plurals.

• changed the y to i and added -es to nouns that end

in a consonant and y.

• remained on topic throughout the paragraph.

Tips for Your Own Writing: Proofreading ....

When you write plural forms, be sure to add -es to words that end in *sh, ch, s, ss,* and *x,* and always change the *y* to *i* before you add -es to make plural words that end in a consonant and *y*.

With these simple rules, you don't have to rely on hunches to make most words plural.

79

Lesson 38

Lesson 38 Usage: Irregular Plurals

Just when you think you know all the rules about making plurals, you'll find there are words that don't follow the rules.

.... **Did You Know?** ....

There are some nouns that do not follow the rules for most plural nouns.

Some nouns have irregular plural forms. These plural nouns do not follow a pattern, so you just have to memorize them.

woman–women   man–men   child–children
foot–feet   goose–geese   ox–oxen
mouse–mice   tooth–teeth   cactus–cacti

For some nouns, the singular and plural forms are the same.

deer–deer   moose–moose   trout–trout
sheep–sheep   series–series salmon–salmon

Show What You Know

Read the following sentences. Write the singular form above each underlined word.

Dad and Uncle Glen are taking a <u>series</u> [series] of fishing classes. They want to
                                1
learn how to catch <u>salmon</u> [salmon]. Last month they went on a fishing trip with
                  2
several other <u>men</u> [man]. Uncle Glen caught five <u>trout</u> [trout]. His <u>feet</u> [foot] were cold from
            3   4   5
standing in the stream for hours. Dad didn't catch anything but two <u>mice</u> [mouse] in
                                                                  6
his tent!

Score: _____   Total Possible: 6

80

Proofread

There are four incorrect plurals in the paragraph below. Use a proofreading mark to delete each underlined word that is incorrect and write the correct plural above it.

Example: Mary lost two ~~tooths~~ [teeth] last night.

Mom invited four ~~womans~~ [women] out to the farm for a picnic. Each one brought
                1
her ~~childs~~ [children]. One child wanted to feed the <u>sheep</u>. Another wanted to pet the
    2   3
~~gooses~~ [geese]. The littlest child dangled his ~~foots~~ [feet] in the pond.
    4   5

Practice

Write a paragraph that tells about the picture. Use the plural forms of nouns when you can.

Review the paragraph to be sure your child has:

• written about the picture.

• used correct plural forms for nouns that have

irregular plurals.

• used the correct plural forms of nouns for which the singular and plural

forms are the same.

Tips for Your Own Writing: Proofreading ....

Sometimes when you write a plural, the word you write does not look right. Keep a dictionary handy to check the spelling of the plural form. Dictionaries show the singular form in bold type and then show the plurals if they are irregular.

Don't get cold feet/foots about forming irregular plurals.

81

Lesson 39

Lesson
39 Usage: Singular Possessives

Singular nouns take apostrophe s ('s) when they show that the noun has or owns something.

.... **Did You Know?** ....

A possessive noun shows ownership or a relationship between two things. An apostrophe (') is always used to mark possessive nouns.

Jane**'s** mountain bike is red.
The windowsill is the cat**'s** favorite place to sleep.

A singular possessive noun shows ownership by one person or thing.

Gary**'s** locker   the principal**'s** office

To make a singular noun possessive, just add **'s**.
the smile of the baby—the baby**'s** smile

....

Show What You Know

On each line below, write the possessive form of the word in parentheses.

1. This is the house that Jack built. Is this ___Jack's___ house? (Jack)

2. Mary has a garden. How does ___Mary's___ garden grow? (Mary)

3. Little Boy Blue, come blow your horn. The ___girl's___ flute broke. (girl)

4. Jack jumped over the candlestick. Did the ___candle's___ flame hurt? (candle)

5. A wise old owl lived in an oak. Is the tree really the ___owl's___ home? (owl)

6. Little Miss Muffet sat on a tuffet. Where was the ___girl's___ chair? (girl)

Score: _____   Total Possible: 6

82

Proofread

Read the paragraph below. There are three apostrophes missing. Use the proper proofreading marks to add an apostrophe to words that show possession.

Example: We are going to Alisha's house after school.

Dad can't find his car keys. He thinks he may have left them in Grandpa's truck. I think he dropped them near Grandma's rosebushes. He has another set of keys, but they are in his boss's car. I said, "Let's look in Mom's purse. You can find anything in there!"

Practice

The animals are having a garage sale to raise money for a new park. Write a paragraph about what each animal has brought to sell. Use singular possessive nouns when you can.

Review the paragraph to be sure your child has:

• used possessive nouns to show ownership.

• added 's to indicate singular possessive nouns.

• written about the suggested topic.

Tips for Your Own Writing: Proofreading ....

Do not confuse plurals and possessives that sound alike, like *dads* and *Dad's*. Remember to use the apostrophe s to make the noun possessive.

When a singular noun is possessive, add a simple 's to it.

83

....

Lesson 40

Lesson
40 Usage: Singular and Plural Possessives

Possessives help you hold your own.

.... **Did You Know?** ....

A singular possessive noun shows ownership by one person or thing.

the **ship's** captain   the **sailor's** uniform

A plural possessive noun shows ownership by more than one person or thing.

the **cities'** streets   the **states'** governors

To make a plural noun that ends in s a possessive noun, add only the apostrophe.

girls—girls**'**   schools—schools**'**

To make a plural noun that does not end in s a possessive noun, add an apostrophe and s.

children—children**'s**   teeth—teeth**'s**

....

Show What You Know

Change the underlined words to include a plural possessive noun. The first one is done for you.

1. The cameras show the faces of the sea otters.   *sea otters' faces*

2. Otters sometimes play by sliding down the slopes of the riverbanks.   *riverbanks' slopes*

3. The mother of pups watches them as they play.   *pups' mother*

4. The mother otter cracks open the shells of sea urchins for food.   *sea urchins' shells*

5. She grooms the coats of the babies to keep them clean and waterproof.   *babies' coats*

Score: _____   Total Possible: 4

84

Proofread

Read the paragraph below. There are four apostrophes and one apostrophe s missing. Use proper proofreading marks to show where they should be added.

Example: The men's tennis match is tomorrow.

During the monthly teachers' meeting, Principal Clark announced that the district would hold an all-schools' camp out on May 24. Highview School would pitch tents in the park. Well, this idea certainly grabbed the students' attention! The boys' campsite would be out near the playground, and the girls' area would be next to the tennis courts. There would be more than 400 kids in the park. Some of the children's parents would be there, too!

Practice

Write a paragraph to describe what is happening in the picture. Use both singular and plural possessive nouns.

Review the paragraph to be sure your child has

written about the picture and has formed and used

singular and plural possessives correctly.

Tips for Your Own Writing: Proofreading ....

When you write plural possessives, you usually add only an apostrophe unless you have a plural that does not end in s, and then you add an apostrophe s.

Children's, not childrens', is the correct plural possessive.

85

Lesson 41

Lesson 41 Usage: Plurals and Possessives

Is it a plural or a possessive? Let the apostrophe be your guide.

.... Did You Know? ....

People are sometimes confused by possessives and plurals because the two forms sound alike, but they are written differently. The possessive form always has an apostrophe. The apostrophe is the signal that means ownership.

> Jeremy collects old *coins*. (plural)
> *Jeremy's* collection was at the library. (singular possessive)
> The *coins'* value increases every year. (plural possessive)

Show What You Know

Read each sentence. If the underlined word means more than one, write *plural* on the line. If it shows ownership, write *possessive.*

1. Millions visit the Grand Canyon yearly. ___plural___

2. Most of them view the canyon from one of the rims. ___plural___

3. The canyon's walls show layers of rock. ___possessive___

4. The earth's forces and erosion formed the Grand Canyon. ___possessive___

5. Guides can answer hikers' questions. ___possessive___

6. The Colorado River's rapids provide exciting raft trips. ___possessive___

7. There are many different trails inside the canyon. ___plural___

8. Beautiful, clear-blue waterfalls roar down the sides of the canyon. ___plural___

Score: _____ Total Possible: 8

86

Proofread

Use proofreading marks to delete three mistakes in plural and possessive forms in the note below. Write the correct word above each mistake.

Example: The ~~runner's~~ runners are in place.

> Dear Mr. Cirillo,
>
> Ted and I really enjoyed going to the rodeo. I liked the
> bucking ~~broncos'~~ broncos best. The ~~riders~~ riders' skills were awesome. Ted
> liked the rodeo clowns. Thanks for one of ~~summers~~ summer's great
> memories!
>
> Sincerely,
>
> *Brian West*

Practice

Write a paragraph describing the animals in the picture. Use both plural and possessive nouns.

Review the paragraph to be sure your child has

described animals in the picture and has used

plural and possessive nouns correctly.

Tips for Your Own Writing: Proofreading ....

If you are not sure whether a word is a plural or a possessive, look to see if a noun comes right after the word. If it does, the word is probably possessive.

A possessive noun must own something.

87

Lesson 42

Lesson 42 Usage: Contractions with *Not*

A contraction is one word that was once two. When you make a contraction, you squeeze together (or contract) the two words into one.

.... Did You Know? ....

A contraction is a shortened form of two words that are joined together. When the words are contracted, some letters are left out. An apostrophe takes the place of the letters that have been left out.

> My bicycle **does not** work.   My bicycle **doesn't** work.

Many contractions are made by putting together a verb and the word *not.*

> did not—did**n't**   are not—are**n't**
> do not—do**n't**   was not—was**n't**
> have not—have**n't**   could not—could**n't**
> has not—has**n't**   should not—should**n't**

Two exceptions are:

> cannot—ca**n't**   will not—wo**n't**

Show What You Know

Write a contraction above the underlined words in each sentence.

We <u>are not</u>^{aren't} smiling. The car <u>will not</u>^{won't} start, and the mechanic <u>cannot</u>^{can't} fix it
until Friday. Antonia <u>could not</u>^{couldn't} go to her piano lesson. Raphael <u>was not</u>^{wasn't} able
to go to baseball practice. I <u>have not</u>^{haven't} gone to the library to work on my
report. We probably <u>should not</u>^{shouldn't} blame "Old Betsy."

Score: _____ Total Possible: 7

88

Proofread

There are five mistakes in contractions in the note below. Use the proper proofreading marks to add apostrophes where they are needed.

Example: They haven't come outside yet.

> Dear Teresa,
>
> I wont be home from work until 7:30 tonight. Dad cant
> make it home early either. Carlito doesnt have a soccer game
> today, so he will be home at about 4:00. Why dont you finish
> your homework together? I didnt plan anything for dinner, so
> we will order pizza when I get home.
>
> Love,
>
> *Mom*

Practice

On another piece of paper, write a letter to a company telling them what you think about one of their products. Describe what you like and dislike about the product.

Review the letter to be sure your child has:
• written a letter with a greeting and a closing.
• written and used contractions correctly.
• written about a product's qualities.

Tips for Your Own Writing: Proofreading ....

Contractions are like shortcuts. You cannot take the shortcut without using an apostrophe. Check your contractions.

Won't is a special contraction. It is formed from the words will and not but is not "willn't."

89

182   Answer Key

Lesson 43

Lesson 43 Usage: Contractions with *Am, Have, Will, Is,* and *Are*

Contractions are a kind of shortcut. Two words are shortened into one.

.... **Did You Know?** ....

Some contractions are formed by joining the words *I, you, she, he, it, we,* or *they* with a verb.

I + am = I'm	we + are = we're
I + have = I've	we + have = we've
he + is = he's	you + are = you're
she + is = she's	they + are = they're
it + is = it's	they + will = they'll
she + will = she'll	

Show What You Know

Write the letter of the words in Column B that matches the contraction in Column A.

Column A	Column B
_g_ **1.** I'm	**a.** you are
_e_ **2.** they're	**b.** I have
_a_ **3.** you're	**c.** we are
_b_ **4.** I've	**d.** it is
_c_ **5.** we're	**e.** they are
_d_ **6.** it's	**f.** she will
_f_ **7.** she'll	**g.** I am

Score: _____   Total Possible: 7

90

Proofread

Read the following paragraph. Use proofreading marks to delete four incorrect contractions and write the correct contraction above each one.

Example: My sister thinks ~~shes~~ she's going to the ball game.

~~Weve~~ We've got tickets to the ice show. You'll be amazed at how the skaters seem to fly over the ice. ~~Ive~~ I've never seen professional skaters before. My brother plays hockey and ~~heis~~ he's a great fan of all ice sports. He'll really appreciate the skaters' skills. He thinks ~~theyll~~ they'll combine both power and style.

Practice

Read about an athlete or another person you admire. Write a paragraph telling about why you admire the person. Use contractions to make your writing sound more natural.

Review the paragraph to be sure your child has:

• written about a person.

• formed and used contractions correctly.

• explained why they admire the person.

Tips for Your Own Writing: Proofreading ....

If you are not sure about where to place the apostrophe, think about the two words that the contraction replaces. Then make sure you place the apostrophe where the letters are missing.

It's a fact! You need an apostrophe when words contract.

91

....

Lesson 44

Lesson 44 Review: Plurals, Possessives, Contractions

A. Write the plural form of each word on the lines below.

1. journey	journeys	**5.** baby	babies
2. brush	brushes	**6.** surprise	surprises
3. box	boxes	**7.** beach	beaches
4. puppy	puppies	**8.** glass	glasses

Score: _____   Total Possible: 8

B. Write the plural form of each word on the lines below.

1. woman	women	**5.** mouse	mice
2. tooth	teeth	**6.** deer	deer
3. man	men	**7.** child	children
4. goose	geese	**8.** moose	moose

Score: _____   Total Possible: 8

C. Add an apostrophe to the four boldface words that show ownership.

A tornado swept through the **streets**₁ of the city last night. A **building's**₂ roof was peeled away. The big oak **trees**₃ leaves were pulled from its branches. Many **cars**₄ were turned over. The **city's**₅ water supply was cut off. Some **roads**₆ were closed. The **library's**₇ windows were shattered.

Score: _____   Total Possible: 4

92

D. Rewrite each of the following phrases on the lines, using a plural possessive.

1. the names of the countries — the countries' names

2. the products of the regions — the regions' products

3. the crops of the farmers — the farmers' crops

4. the jobs of the workers — the workers' jobs

Score: _____   Total Possible: 4

E. Circle the correct form of the word in each sentence below.

The ((teams)₁ teams') were ready to race. Each (schools, (school's)₂) team wore a different color. The ((runners)₃ runner's) began to line up. Where were (Rosas, (Rosa's)₄) shoes? ((Whistles)₅ Whistle's) began to blow!

Score: _____   Total Possible: 5

F. Read each sentence below. On the lines below, write the two words that make up each of the four underlined contractions.

1. Some people <u>don't</u> follow basic safety rules. — do not

2. Children <u>shouldn't</u> play on busy streets. — should not

3. Jim <u>didn't</u> look both ways before crossing the highway. — did not

4. Aaron <u>wasn't</u> wearing his seat belt. — was not

Score: _____   Total Possible: 4

G. Write the contraction for the underlined words above each.

I've
<u>I have</u>₁ invited ten friends to a pizza party. We'll
<u>We will</u>₂ order pizza. We're
<u>We are</u>₃ going to eat outside. It's
<u>It is</u>₄ nice to finally have warm weather.

Score: _____   Total Possible: 4

REVIEW SCORE: _____   REVIEW TOTAL: 37

93

Lesson 45

Lesson 45 — Usage: Regular Verb Tense

Verbs change to show the past because today becomes yesterday so fast.

.... **Did You Know?** ....

Tense is a word that means "time." The tense of a verb tells you when the action takes place.

A verb in the *present tense* shows action that happens now.

The soccer players **kick** the ball toward the net.

A verb in the *past tense* shows action that already happened. Add *-ed* to form the past tense of most verbs.

The soccer players **kicked** the ball toward the net.

To form the past tense of verbs that end in *e*, drop the *e* and add *-ed.*

rake—rak**ed**　　place—plac**ed**　　taste—tast**ed**

Show What You Know

Write the past tense of the verb in parentheses.

1. We ___walked___ to the movies. (walk)

2. We didn't know that Len's dog ___followed___ us. (follow)

3. We didn't notice that people ___pointed___ at us. (point)

4. We finally ___turned___ around. (turn)

5. Skipper ___carried___ a dollar bill in his mouth. (carry)

Score: _____　Total Possible: 5

94

Proofread

There are four mistakes in verb tense in the paragraph below. Use proper proofreading marks to add *-ed* to show action that has already happened. In one mistake, you must drop an e before you add the *-ed.*

Example: He tast~~e~~ᵉᵈ lobster for the first time yesterday.

In 1497, Amerigo Vespucci sailᵉᵈ to a new land. He callᵉᵈ it *Mundus Novus*, which means "New World" in Latin. Many years later, a German geographer decid~~e~~ᵉᵈ to name the new land *America* after Amerigo Vespucci. The new land was South America. Later, North America, where Viking explorers first landᵉᵈ in about A.D. 1000, was also named after Amerigo Vespucci.

Practice

Write a paragraph about an explorer you know about. When you are finished writing, reread your paragraph to check for the proper spelling of past tense verbs.

Review the paragraph to be sure your child has:

* written about an explorer.

* formed the past tense of regular verbs by adding *-ed.*

* formed the past tense of regular verbs that end in *e* by dropping the *e* and adding *-ed.*

* stayed on the topic throughout the paragraph.

Tips for Your Own Writing: Proofreading ....

Make sure that if you write about something that has already happened, you use the past tense of the verbs.

Don't let verbs make you tense!

95

....

Lesson 46

Lesson 46 — Usage: Irregular Verb Tense

Irregular verbs break the rules!

.... **Did You Know?** ....

Some verbs are special. They do not end in *-ed* to show past time. These verbs are called *irregular verbs* because they do not follow the pattern for forming the past tense. They have one special spelling to show past time.

Erica **takes** us to the city each month. (present)
Last month, she **took** us to the art museum. (past)
We usually **ride** the train to the city. (present)
On our last trip, we **rode** the bus. (past)

Other irregular verbs include:

break—broke	begin—began	come—came
do—did	draw—drew	eat—ate
make—made	think—thought	write—wrote
say—said	catch—caught	run—ran
grow—grew	win—won	give—gave
spring—sprung	buy—bought	

Show What You Know

Write the past tense of the verb over each underlined irregular verb in the sentences below.

Julio ran~~run~~ in a 5K race last week. He thought~~think~~ that he would win. Tanya came~~come~~ from behind and caught~~catch~~ up with Julio. Tanya passed him and won~~win~~ the race. She broke~~break~~ the school record. Julio did~~do~~ not feel bad about losing the race. He said~~say~~ he will try harder next time.

Score: _____　Total Possible: 8

96

Proofread

Read the paragraph below. Use proofreading marks to delete six incorrect verbs in the sentences and write the correct verb above each one.

Example: Todd caught~~catch~~ the biggest fish.

Last year, Samantha grew~~grow~~ pumpkins in the garden. She gave~~give~~ one to Linda. Linda took~~take~~ the pumpkin home. She drew a face on the pumpkin. Her mom made~~make~~ a pumpkin pie. Linda ate~~eat~~ the seeds. Then she wrote~~write~~ Samantha a thank-you note.

Practice

You have a green thumb and your vegetables are huge! Write a paragraph about your garden. Use the past tense of *grow, give, spring, begin,* and *buy.*

Review the paragraph to be sure your child has

written about a vegetable garden and has

correctly used irregular past tenses of the verbs

listed above.

Tips for Your Own Writing: Proofreading ....

Saying the past tense aloud can help you decide whether the verb takes *-ed* to form the past tense or is irregular. *Sitted* just does not sound right!

If you are not sure about the past tense of a verb, look it up in a dictionary.

97

Lesson 47

Lesson

47 Usage: Verb Agreement

Do you ever wear a winter coat and a bathing suit together? Parts of a sentence have to "go together" just as your clothes do.

.... **Did You Know?** ....

The verb has to agree with the subject of the sentence. This means that they must both be either singular or plural.

Usually if the subject is singular, or the pronoun *he, she,* or *it,* add -s or -es to the verb.

> Dad **remembers** when few homes had TV sets.
> He often **reads** to the class.

If the subject is more than one, or the pronoun *I, you, we,* or *they,* do <u>not</u> add -s or -es to the verb.

> My parents always **watch** the news on TV.
> I **ride** my bike to school.

....

Show What You Know
Write the verb on the line that correctly completes each sentence.

1. Adam __works__ on the new computer. (works, work)

2. He __uses__ it to do his homework. (use, uses)

3. His brothers __play__ games on it. (plays, play)

4. His mom __writes__ stories on it. (writes, write)

5. His sister __types__ reports for school. (type, types)

6. Computers __make__ many jobs easier. (makes, make)

Score: _____ Total Possible: 6

98

Proofread
Read the paragraph below. There are five mistakes in subject-verb agreement. Use a proofreading mark to delete each incorrect word and write the correct word above it.

Example: Jessica ~~talk~~ on the phone too long. [talks]

The birth of a baby elephant at the zoo is an exciting event. Soon after it is born, the baby ~~wobble~~ to its feet. Its mother ~~nudge~~ it to take its first steps. The thirsty baby ~~drink~~ its mother's milk. The older elephants stroke it with their trunks to welcome it to the herd. Mama elephant ~~teach~~ it to use its trunk to drink and grab food. She even ~~show~~ it how to squirt showers of water over itself. [wobbles, nudges, drinks, teaches, shows]

Practice
Add verbs to sentences 1 and 3. Add subjects to sentences 2 and 4. Make sure each subject and verb work together.

1. Mountain hikers __Review each sentence to make sure the subject and verb agree.__

2. _____ appears in the distance.

3. A family of bears _____.

4. _____ block the trail.

Tips for Your Own Writing: Proofreading ....
Let your ears be the judge of whether the parts of the sentence agree with each other. Read what you write out loud.

Subjects and verbs should always agree.

99

....

Lesson 48

Lesson

48 Review: Verbs

A. Each sentence shows present time. Use proofreading marks to change the eight underlined verbs to show past time. Write the past tense of the verb above each underlined word.

Officer Jane <u>comes</u> to speak to our class. She <u>brings</u> safety posters. She <u>talks</u> about bicycle and playground safety. She <u>helps</u> us write some safety rules of our own. Our teacher <u>shows</u> us a film about school bus safety. Then we <u>tour</u> the police station. We <u>ask</u> Captain Jarvis about traffic safety. He <u>offers</u> us a ride in his police car. [came, brought, talked, helped, showed, toured, asked, offered]

Score: _____ Total Possible: 8

B. Write the correct verb to complete each sentence.

1. Astronauts often __go__ up in space today. (go, went)

2. Some people once __thought__ space travel was impossible. (think, thought)

3. In the 1960s, Neil Armstrong __flew__ in *Apollo II*. (fly, flew)

4. He actually __stood__ on the surface of the moon. (stand, stood)

5. He __brought__ moon rocks back to Earth. (bring, brought)

6. Reporters __wrote__ many stories about the lunar landing. (write, wrote)

7. Millions of Americans __saw__ the moon landing on TV. (see, saw)

8. Today astronauts no longer __fly__ to the moon. (fly, flew)

9. Now they __take__ the space shuttle to and from space. (take, took)

Score: _____ Total Possible: 9

100

C. Write the past tense of each verb on the line.

1. The itsy-bitsy spider climb up the water spout. __climbed__

2. Down come the rain. __came__

3. It wash the spider out. __washed__

4. Out come the sun. __came__

5. It dry up all the rain. __dried__

6. The itsy-bitsy spider crawl up the spout again. __crawled__

Score: _____ Total Possible: 6

D. Write the correct form of the word in parentheses to complete each sentence.

1. The bus __is__ late this morning. (is, are)

2. We __wait__ at the corner. (wait, waits)

3. Dad __offers__ to drive us to school. (offers, offer)

4. The traffic signal __breaks__ on the highway. (breaks, break)

5. We __board__ the bus at the last minute. (boards, board)

6. Our teacher, Ms. Kerr, __waits__ outside. (waits, wait)

Score: _____ Total Possible: 6

E. Write a present tense verb that agrees with each subject.

1. (to buy) She __buys__   4. (to wear) He __wears__

2. (to see) I __see__   5. (to carry) They __carry__

3. (to cry) Bill __cries__   6. (to lean) It __leans__

Score: _____ Total Possible: 6

REVIEW SCORE: _____ REVIEW TOTAL: 35

101

Lesson 49

Lesson
49 Usage: Subject-Pronoun Agreement

✎ *What do pronouns replace? They replace nouns or other pronouns.*

························· **Did You Know?** ·························

A pronoun is a word that can take the place of one or more nouns or pronouns in a sentence.

Franklin was a printer. **He** was also a writer.

Subject pronouns are used as subjects in a sentence. Subjects are the persons or things that do whatever is being done in the sentence.

I, you, he, she, and ***it*** are subject pronouns that mean only one.

I saw Henri. **He** was with Sam.

You, we, and ***they*** are subject pronouns that mean more than one.

Jill and I are friends. **We** are close.

When you use *I* with another noun or pronoun, you should put *I* last.

Liu and I went to the library.

···

Show What You Know

Read each sentence below. Circle the five subject pronouns.

What do (you) know about Sally Ride? (She) was the first female astronaut in the U.S. space program. In 1983 Sally rocketed into space on a space shuttle. (It) was named *Challenger.* (She) and John Fabian operated the shuttle's robotic arm. (They) used it to launch and retrieve satellites.

Score: _____   Total Possible: 5

102

Proofread

On the line, write a pronoun to take the place of the underlined word or words in each sentence.

Example: <u>John</u> worked on the committee, and ___he___ also decorated.

<u>Kyle and Karen</u> wanted to earn money because ___they___ wanted to go to
                                                        1
summer camp. <u>Kyle</u> made flyers, and ___he___ gave the flyers to all the
                                           2
neighbors. <u>The flyers</u> read: "Lawn Mowing, $6 each yard," and ___they___
                                                                     3
listed Kyle's phone number. <u>Mr. Karres, Ms. Blumberg, and I</u> called the
number on the flyers, and ___we___ asked Kyle to mow our lawns. Later, I
                           4
saw the <u>flyer</u> Karen made, and ___it___ read: "Dogs walked twice a day for
                                      5
$10 a week." I called <u>Karen</u> in the morning, and ___she___ came to meet my
                                                        6
dog. Now <u>Karen and Kyle</u> both work for me, and ___they___ do an excellent job.
                                                     7

Practice

Talk with your friends about a way you can earn money next summer. Then on another piece of paper, write a flyer to describe your services and fees. Use subject pronouns when you can.

Review the flyer to be sure your child has described services and fees and has used singular and plural subject pronouns correctly.

Tips for Your Own Writing: Revising ·················

Do you want to avoid repeating a subject noun over and over again in your writing? If so, replace the noun with a subject pronoun. Remember to let your reader know who or what the pronoun refers to.

✎ *Use a pronoun correctly by making it clear what it replaces.*

103

Lesson 50

Lesson
50 Usage: Object-Pronoun Agreement

✎ *Pronouns are good stand-ins for nouns. Learn when and how to use pronouns to get the job done!*

························· **Did You Know?** ·························

A pronoun is a word that can take the place of one or more nouns or other pronouns in a sentence.

Carl gave the ball to Lou, and Lou dropped the **ball.**
Carl gave the ball to Lou, and Lou dropped **it.**

Object pronouns follow action verbs and words like *to, for, at, of,* and *with. Me, you, him, her,* and *it* are used when you are writing about a singular object.

Hector gave **me** a piñata from Mexico.
Did Hector buy one for **you?**

Us, you, and ***them*** are used when you are talking about a plural object.

Mai called Jim and me to ask **us** to the movies.
We always have a good time with **them.**

···

Show What You Know

Write the correct pronoun in each blank.

1. Jeff was teaching Rita and ___me___ how to play tennis. (I, me)

2. He showed ___us___ over and over again how to hold our rackets. (we, us)

3. Rita said it was too awkward for ___her___. (she, her)

4. Hitting the balls was a problem for ___me___. (me, I)

5. I spent a lot of time chasing after ___them___! (them, they)

Score: _____   Total Possible: 5

104

Proofread

There are five mistakes in the use of object pronouns in the paragraph below. Use a proofreading mark to delete each incorrect pronoun and write the correct pronoun above it.

Example: Jessica couldn't find ~~he~~.
                                    him

Dad read nursery rhymes to my sister and ~~I~~ when we were young. Each of
                                           me
~~we~~ had a favorite rhyme. My sister liked "Jack and Jill." Dad must have read it
 us
to her 1,000 times! I also liked it, but my favorite one was "Three Little
Kittens." That rhyme is about kittens who lost their mittens and couldn't find
~~they~~. I don't ask Dad to read to ~~I~~ anymore. Now I ask if I can read to ~~he~~.
them   me   him

Practice

Write a paragraph about something you do with someone in your family. As you write, use object pronouns to avoid repeating the same noun.

Review the paragraph to be sure your child has:

• used object pronouns after verbs and prepositions.

• used *me, you, him, her,* or *it* when writing about a singular object.

• used *us, you,* or *them* when writing about a plural object.

• written about one or more activities they enjoy doing with family members.

Tips for Your Own Writing: Proofreading ·················

Remember that object pronouns follow action verbs and words like *to* and *of.* Check that the pronouns you use as objects are *me, it, him, her, us, you,* and *them.*

✎ *Object pronouns can be used in place of nouns used as objects.*

105

Lesson 51

Lesson 51 Usage: Double Negatives

Should you ever use double negatives? No, not never!

············· **Did You Know?** ·············

Sometimes when you write a sentence, you use a negative word like *no*. *None, nothing, never,* and *no one* are also negative words.

> Rob will **never** weed the garden.
> **None** of the yard work was finished.

The word *not* and contractions made with *not* are also negatives.

> I did **not** water the plants.   He **won't** rake the leaves.

Only one negative word is needed in a sentence.

There are two ways to correct a double negative. A positive word can replace a negative word, or the *n't* can be dropped.

> **Incorrect:** There **weren't no** books on the shelf.
> **Correct:** There **weren't any** books on the shelf *or* there **were no** books on the shelf.

Show What You Know
Complete each sentence by writing the correct word in the blank.

1. Most people __will__ never get caught in a fire. (will, won't)

2. Never store __any__ paint in open cans. (no, any)

3. Don't __ever__ use gasoline to start a bonfire or grill. (never, ever)

4. Never leave __a__ candle or fire unattended. (a, no)

Score: _____   Total Possible: 4

106

Proofread
There are four double negatives in the note below. Use proofreading marks to delete the double negatives and write the corrections above them.

Example: Sarah ~~doesn't never~~ want to go there again. *(doesn't ever)*

> Dear Hugh,
> I ~~won't never~~ pick flowers in the woods again. There *(won't ever/will never)*
> ~~wasn't no~~ warning sign. How was I to know what poison ivy *(wasn't any/was no)*
> looked like? ~~No one never~~ told me about it. There isn't any *(No one ever)*
> way to get rid of it. ~~Nothing won't~~ stop the itching! *(Nothing will)*
>
> Your rash-covered friend,
>
> *Matt*

Practice
Make up a list of good manners. Write sentences using the words *no, never, nothing,* or *none* or sentences with negative contractions.

> *Review the list of rules to be sure your child has used only one negative word in a*
> *sentence that gives a negative message.*

Tips for Your Own Writing: Proofreading ·············
You always want to avoid having two negatives in one sentence. When you check your writing, if there is more than one, get rid of one.

Never, no never say, "I don't have no homework!"

107

··

Lesson 52

Lesson 52 Review: Pronouns and Double Negatives

A. On each blank, write a subject pronoun that could refer to the underlined words.

Christine and I are in the same Explorer Troop, and __we__ went on a *(1)* rafting trip together. Christine asked me if __I__ was afraid. This was *(2)* Christine's first rafting trip, and __she__ was a little bit frightened. The *(3)* guides said that __they__ always followed the safety rules and would watch *(4)* us carefully. The guides were right about the trip down the river. __It__ *(5)* was very exciting, and no one got hurt.

Score: _____   Total Possible: 5

B. On each blank, write an object pronoun that refers to the underlined word(s).

Dad asked if my sister and I wanted to go to work with __him__. Ariella *(1)* and I jumped at the chance to see the factory, and so on Friday Dad took __us__ there. As we walked through the assembly line, Dad explained how *(2)* __it__ worked. I watched Dad work on the line, and he showed __me__ *(3)* *(4)* how to use a drill to tighten bolts. Just then a whistle blew. All the workers grabbed their lunches, and we followed __them__ to the lunchroom. We ate *(5)* lunch and then Dad took us home. Ariella and I had a great time at the factory, and we hope Dad will take __us__ there again. *(6)*

Score: _____   Total Possible: 6

108

C. Write the eleven correct pronouns in the following paragraphs.

One of the three little pigs said to the others, "__We__ need to build new *(1)(We, Us)* houses." Each of __them__ built a new house. __They__ used different *(2)(they, them)* *(3)(They, Them)* materials to build their houses. Millie Pig told them not to use straw or sticks to build their houses, but two of __them__ didn't listen to __her__. *(4)(they, them)* *(5)(she, her)*

When the wolf came, __he__ easily blew down the houses that had *(6)(he, him)* been built of straw and sticks. Then the wolf went to the one brick house and said, "Open up, or __I__ will blow your house down." Of course, __he__ *(7)(I, me)* *(8)(he, him)* couldn't blow it down, and so the wolf slid down the chimney. The pig had a surprise for __him__, though. __He__ landed in a pot of boiling water. That *(9)(he, him)* *(10)(He, Him)* old wolf jumped out of the pot and ran away. __He__ never bothered the *(11)(He, Him)* pigs again.

Score: _____   Total Possible: 11

D. Read the paragraph below. Use proper proofreading marks to delete five incorrect bold words and write the correct word above each one.

I don't really **~~never~~** like to clean my room. Cleaning isn't **~~nothing~~** I would *(ever)(1)* *(anything)(2)* choose to do. Dad said that I didn't have **~~no~~** choice. I had to clean my room, *(any)(3)* or I couldn't invite anyone over to the house. He said that I could have **~~anyone~~** over to see this mess. Yes, I cleaned my room, and I promised that I *(no one)(4)* wouldn't **~~never~~** leave it in such a mess again. *(ever)(5)*

Score: _____   Total Possible: 5

REVIEW SCORE: _____   REVIEW TOTAL: 27

109

Lesson 53

Lesson 53 Grammar: Nouns

Imagine a circus in your mind. Can you see the clowns, tigers, and tightrope walkers? Do you smell the popcorn and cotton candy? Nouns are words that make pictures in the reader's mind.

.... **Did You Know?** ....

A *noun* is a word that tells who or what did the action or was acted upon in the sentence.

The **ringmaster** wore a tall, shiny, black **hat**.

A *common noun* names any person or place.

woman   mountain   school

A *singular noun* names one person, place, or thing and a *plural noun* names more than one.

singular—town   plural—towns

A *proper noun* names a particular person or place. Proper nouns start with capital letters.

Eleanor Roosevelt   Southside School

A *possessive noun* names who or what owns something.

Pedro's basketball   the dog's bone   the actor's role

Show What You Know

Circle the common nouns in the following paragraph. Underline the proper nouns.

(Dodoes) once lived on the (island) of Mauritius in the Indian Ocean. (Dodoes) were very unusual (birds) Their (wings) were very tiny, so (dodoes) could not fly. A (dodo) was as big as a large (turkey) These (birds) no longer exist.

Score: _____   Total Possible: 11

110

Practice

Replace the underlined common noun in each sentence with a proper noun. Write the proper noun above the common noun.

Example: Some students in <u>the school</u> are [Lincoln Elementary School] interested in astronomy.

Sample answers are given.

<u>Two girls</u> [Tenisha and Marta] from our class went on a trip to the planetarium. The planetarium was in <u>the city</u> [Chicago]. <u>One girl</u> [Tenisha] asked a question about <u>a planet</u> [Jupiter]. <u>The other girl</u> [Marta] was reading a book. It was about <u>an astronaut</u> [Sally Ride]. The astronaut flew on the <u>space shuttle</u> [Challenger]. Returning from space, the shuttle landed in <u>a state</u> [California]. The astronaut met <u>the President</u> [President Reagan].

Revise

Write another noun above each underlined noun to make the paragraph more interesting.

Sample answers are given.

Have you ever visited a pet <u>place</u> [shop]? If you have, then you know there are many kinds of <u>things</u> [pets] for sale there. In the window, you might see some frisky <u>animals</u> [puppies]. In hanging cages, you might notice some colorful <u>birds</u> [parakeets]. No doubt you would see <u>containers</u> [tanks] filled with <u>animals</u> [fish]. In smaller cages, you might see some <u>animals</u> [mice] running around on a wheel.

Tips for Your Own Writing: Revising ....

Choose a piece of your own writing. Underline the nouns. Check that you used the best noun in each position. Using a specific common noun or proper nouns can add information and interest to your sentences.

The name's the thing! Choosing the best noun for the job will make your writing more interesting.

111

Lesson 54

Lesson 54 Grammar: Pronouns

What did the pronoun say to the noun? Anything you can do I can do, too!

.... **Did You Know?** ....

A *pronoun* is a word that takes the place of a noun or nouns. They help you avoid using the same nouns over and over. Pronouns change their spelling according to their use.

John said that **John** was going to ride **John's** bike.

John said that **he** was going to ride **his** bike.

I, you, she, and *they* are examples of <u>subject pronouns.</u>

Squanto was a member of the Pawtuxet tribe.

He was a member of the Pawtuxet tribe.

Me, him, us, and *them* are examples of <u>object pronouns.</u>

Squanto showed the **colonists** how to fish.

Squanto showed **them** how to fish.

My, your, and *their* are examples of <u>possessive pronouns.</u>

Squanto's friendship was important.

His friendship was important.

Show What You Know

Circle the pronouns in the sentences below.

Have (you) ever heard of Jane Addams? (She) wanted to help people living in poverty. There were no government agencies to help (them) Addams established a settlement house in Chicago. (It) was a place to receive help and learn new skills. The settlement house helped many people and made (their) lives easier.

Score: _____   Total Possible: 5

112

Practice

Write a pronoun in each of the blanks so that the paragraph makes sense. Sample answers are given.

Four little ducklings pecked __their__ [1] way out of __their__ [2] eggs. Mother Duck watched excitedly as __her__ [3] babies climbed out of the shells. When the time came, Mother Duck waddled out of __her__ [4] nest. __She__ [5] quacked to her ducklings. __They__ [6] followed Mother Duck as __she__ [7] headed for the pond. One by one the ducklings followed __her__ [8] into the water. __They__ [9] all swam happily together around the pond.

Revise

Each underlined pronoun in the paragraph below is incorrect. Write the correct pronoun above each underlined word.

Do you like tomatoes? Did <u>we</u> [you] [1] know that at one time almost everyone in the United States thought <u>them</u> [they] [2] were poisonous? People grew tomatoes in <u>them</u> [their] [3] gardens only because <u>his</u> [their] [4] fruit was pretty. There is a story that one day a man took some tomatoes to town and offered <u>him</u> [them] [5] to the people who passed by. No one would touch <u>their</u> [them] [6]. So the man ate <u>it</u> [them] [7] all up. <u>She</u> [He] [8] did not die. The news spread. <u>I</u> [It] [9] helped people change <u>them</u> [their] [10] minds about tomatoes.

Tips for Your Own Writing: Revising ....

When you speak, you can use a lot of pronouns because you can point to people and things. When you write, make sure your pronouns point to nouns.

Pronouns make sense when they clearly refer to someone or something.

113

Lesson 55

Lesson 55 — Grammar: Verbs

The game is tied. Michael Jordan runs, jumps, shoots, and scores! Bulls win! Bulls win! A verb is the action word in a sentence.

.... **Did You Know?** ....

A *verb* is a word that shows action or expresses a state of being. Every sentence must have a verb. A verb such as *Go!* can be a one-word sentence. *Jump, shoot, listen,* and *read* are action verbs.
Am, are, is, was, were, be, being, and *been* are all forms of the verb *be.* They tell what someone or something is, was, or will be.
A *present tense* verb shows action that happens now.
   The farmer **plants** corn in early spring.
A *past tense* verb shows action that happened earlier.
   The farmer **planted** beans in that field last year.
A *future tense* verb shows action that will happen.
   Next year, the farmer **will plant** barley.
....

Show What You Know

Underline the ten verbs in the paragraph below. Write *present, past,* or *future* above each verb to tell when the action takes place.

        present
There is an ancient Greek legend about a nine-headed dragon that lived in
            past   past
a lake. The dragon attacked sailing ships. Many people said, "Kill the dragon."
          past   past   future
Each time one head was cut off, another head grew in its place. Hercules
  past   past   past
solved the problem. He cut off each head and sealed the neck with fire.

                                    Score: _____   Total Possible: 20

114

Practice

Write a verb in each blank. You can make the paragraph interesting with the verbs you choose. Sample answers are given.

   A zoo is a fun place to ___visit___. People ___watch___ the way
                           1   2
animals ___move___. Monkeys ___climb___ up rocks or ___jump___
         3   4   5
from tree to tree chasing other monkeys. In the reptile house,
snakes ___crawl___ down tree trunks.
        6
Their tongues ___flick___ in and out. The
               7
slow-moving elephants ___walk___ over
                       8
to the water in their pen and fill their trunks.
Then they arch their trunks over their
heads and ___spray___ the water all
            9
over their bodies to stay cool.

Revise

Write a more interesting verb above each underlined verb.
Sample answers are given.

                                 roamed
   Woolly mammoths walked on Earth more than three million years ago.
                    1
       grew   looked
These creatures were about eleven feet tall. They seemed like hairy elephants.
              2   3
        ate   hunted
Mammoths had moss, grass, and twigs. Early humans killed the woolly
          4   5
mammoth for food and clothing. The last woolly mammoths ended about ten
                                         died   6
thousand years ago.

Review the paragraphs to be sure your child has used verbs to show action or express state of being correctly and has used verbs that make sense.

Tips for Your Own Writing: Revising ....

In your own story writing, check that your verbs are in the appropriate tense: past tense, present tense, or future tense.

You're really taking some action when you use verbs!

115

....

Lesson 56

Lesson 56 — Grammar: Adjectives

You've just come home, and you're starving. On the kitchen table is a basket filled with crisp, red apples, golden-yellow bananas, and juicy, ripe peaches. See how adjectives can add flavor to your writing!

.... **Did You Know?** ....

An *adjective* is a word that describes a noun or pronoun. *Crisp, red, golden-yellow, juicy,* and *ripe* describe the fruit in the sentence above.
Adjectives tell a reader *what kind* and *how many.*
   Clouds can be **soft, fluffy, threatening,** or **black.**
Adjectives usually come before the nouns they describe but can come after the verb.
   crying baby   **six** balloons   **sour** pickle
An adjective is a word that can fit in both these blanks: The _____ tree is very _____.
   The **tall** tree is very **tall.**
....

Show What You Know

Circle the fifteen adjectives in the paragraph below.

On a (crisp), (cool) evening, Donna, a (young) (Alaskan) girl, was watching
television. A (short) message flashed across the screen: "(Great) auroras out
tonight." Donna pulled on her (warm) parka and went outside. (Twin) pathways
of (greenish-white) light arced across the (dark) sky. As Donna watched the
(shining) trail, a (red) border grew along its (bottom) edge. Suddenly the ball of
light exploded, shooting (colorful) rays in (many) directions.

                                    Score: _____   Total Possible: 15

116

Practice

Write an adjective on each blank. Two are shown as examples.

   On a vacation, a family played a game called "I Spy." Each person described
something he or she saw. Then they repeated what everyone else had seen,
but they changed the words that described each thing. Here is their game:
                                      Sample answers are given.
   "I spy ___blue___ water."
   "I spy a ___giant___ whale and ___choppy___ water."
   "I spy a ___black___ dog, a ___gray___ whale,
and ___smooth___ water."
   "I spy some ___pretty___ wildflowers, a
___friendly___ dog, a ___baby___ whale, and ___clear___
water."

Revise

Write a more descriptive adjective above each of the underlined adjectives in the following paragraph.
Sample answers are given.

   When Sara decided to join the band, she had to choose an instrument to
                                     brassy   noisy
play. Would she pick a big trumpet? How about a loud bass drum? Sara
                          1   2
             mellow   deep
always liked the nice sound of the flute. She also liked the low, rumbling
                   3   4
            wonderful
sound of the tuba. There were so many good instruments that it was hard to
                                        5
decide. What do you think she chose?

Tips for Your Own Writing: Revising ....

Check a story you have written. Make sure you have placed your adjectives before the nouns or after verbs like *be* and *feel.*

Terrific, stupendous, *and* wonderful—all are adjectives that describe good work.

117

Lesson 57

Lesson
57 Grammar: Adverbs

We went to the beginners' band concert. Some students played well, others played enthusiastically, and a few played badly.

.... **Did You Know?** ....

Adverbs can describe verbs. They tell *when, where,* **or** *how* **an action happens.**

The concert will start **soon.** (*Soon* tells when.)
The tuba player sits **here.** (*Here* tells where.)
The drummer plays **loudly.** (*Loudly* tells how.)

Adverbs can describe adjectives. They usually answer the question *how or to what degree.*

quite handsome   **too** small   **rather** sweet

My **really** naughty dog chews **very** old slippers. How naughty is my dog? *Really* naughty. How old are the slippers? *Very* old.

Adverbs can also describe other adverbs.

very quickly   **extremely** slowly   **awfully** quietly

Show What You Know
Circle the adverb that describes the verb in bold type. Then circle the question that the adverb answers.

1. The game **started** (early) in the afternoon.   How? (When?) Where?
2. The Bombers (confidently) **took** the field.   (How?) When? Where?
3. The batter **walked** (slowly) to home plate.   (How?) When? Where?
4. The pitcher **threw** (there.)   How? When? (Where?)
5. The batter (easily) **hit** the ball.   (How?) When? Where?
6. The crowd **applauded** (loudly.)   (How?) When? Where?

Score: _____   Total Possible: 12

118

Practice
Write adverbs on the blank lines to describe the verbs in each sentence.
Sample answers are given.

Mr. Walsh ___completely___ described the science
                           1
experiments to the class. Robbie ___happily___
                                       2
volunteered to grow crystals. He filled a jar
with water, and ___next___ added sugar. He
                      3
tied a string to a pencil and suspended it in the
water. ___Then___ , he put the jar in the
            4
sunlight. Each morning he ___eagerly___ checked
                                 5
the jar. ___Finally___ , a few small specks appeared
              6
on the string. Robbie reported ___proudly___ that his experiment was working!
                                      7

Revise
Adverbs add details to your writing. Different adverbs can be used to change the meanings of sentences. Replace the underlined adverbs. Write your adverbs above the underlined ones.
Sample answers are given.

                                                    beautifully
Birthday parties are so much fun. Guests come bringing nicely wrapped
                                                        1
        excitedly   loudly
gifts. During the games, everyone cheers happily. They sing strongly as the
                                            2   3
         quickly   brightly
cake's candles are rapidly lit. The candles shine wonderfully, while everyone
                        4   5
       silently   cheerfully
waits noiselessly for the wish. Later we talk loudly as the gifts are opened,
          6   7
                          carefully
and each one is lifted slowly out of its box. Review to make sure your child has added
                          8
variety and has written adverbs that make sense.

Tips for Your Own Writing: Revising ....
Look at a report you have written. Would your report be better if you added adverbs that tell when, where, and how?

Surely, you can tell that all adverbs describe verbs, adjectives, or other adverbs well.

119

Lesson 58

Lesson
58 Grammar: Articles

Little words can make a big difference. Good writers pay attention to all details, big and small.

.... **Did You Know?** ....

A, an, **and** *the* **are useful words called** underlined(articles)**. You can think of them as noun signals. They tell the reader there is a noun coming in the sentence.**
A **and** *an* **tell about any person, place, thing, or idea. Use** *a* **with nouns that start with a consonant.**

a ball   **a** jump rope   **a** zebra

Use *an* **with nouns that start with a vowel sound.**

an egg   **an** oyster   **an** umbrella

The **tells about a specific person, place, thing, or idea.**

Give me **the** apple, please.

Show What You Know
Underline each word in the sentences below that signals any person, place, thing, or idea. Circle each word that signals a specific person, place, thing, or idea.

We took my brother Jim to college last week. I had never been to a_ big university before. (The) campus was as big as a_ small town. Jim has classes in several different buildings. We visited a_ science building and (the) library. (The) dormitory where Jim lives is a_ ten-story building. (The) cafeteria and study rooms are on (the) first floor. (The) computer lab is on (the) fifth floor.

Score: _____   Total Possible: 11

120

Practice
Choose the article that best completes each sentence below. Write the articles in the blanks. Sample answers are given.

What if you were on ___a___ deserted
                          1
island and you wanted fruit to eat? You couldn't
buy it at ___a___ grocery store. You would have
              2
to find it. You will first need to know if ___the___
                                                3
fruit is safe to eat. ___The___ red fruit looks safe.
                          4
What about ___the___ yellow fruit, ___the___ white fruit, or ___a___ bunch of
                5   6   7
green ones? Can you pick between ___a___ green or ___a___ yellow piece
                                        8   9
of fruit? How about ___an___ orange fruit? This should be ___an___ easy
                          10   11
choice.

Revise
Read each underlined article below. If it is not correct, write the correct article above each underlined one.

  An
  A animal's tail can come in handy in many ways. An horse can use its tail
  1   2
                           a   the
to chase away an insect. An tail of the fish is used to push it through a
        3   4   5   6
         A   A
water. An monkey hangs by its tail so that its hands are free to find food. An
        7   8
         a
beaver smacks its tail on a water when danger is near. A skunk raises its tail
                          9   10
as the warning that it is about to spray.
      11

Tips for Your Own Writing: Revising ....
Check your writing to make sure you have used *a* and *an* correctly. *A* is used when a word begins with a consonant sound, and *an* is used when a word begins with a vowel sound.

A word and the *word are two very different words, indeed!*

121

Lesson 59

Lesson 59 Review: Parts of Speech

A. Read the paragraph below. Underline sixteen nouns.

<u>Harriet Tubman</u> was born a <u>slave</u> in 1820 in <u>Maryland</u>. She escaped from a <u>plantation</u> in 1849 but had to leave her <u>family</u> behind. <u>Harriet</u> wanted <u>freedom</u> for her <u>people</u>. She helped hide <u>slaves</u> who were on their way to <u>Canada</u>. She was <u>one</u> of the famous <u>conductors</u> on the <u>Underground Railroad</u>. Her <u>bravery</u> helped lead more than 300 <u>people</u> to <u>freedom</u>.

Score: _____   Total Possible: 16

B. Replace the word or words in bold type with a pronoun. Write the pronoun above the bold word.

Kay rides home on the six o'clock train. Every day **Kay** [she, 1] meets Bill on the train. Kay and Bill give the conductor **Kay's and Bill's** [their, 2] tickets, and **the conductor** [he/she, 3] checks **the tickets** [them, 4]. When the train departs, **the train** [it, 5] is almost full. The conductor talks to Bill and helps **Bill** [him, 6] put **Bill's** [his, 7] briefcase on the shelf.

Score: _____   Total Possible: 7

C. Underline the verb in each sentence. Write a more vivid verb above each one. You can use a verb from the list below.

unlocked	walked	escaped	will sleep
searched	raced	returned	ate

The zookeeper <u>went</u> [walked] over to the monkey's cage. He <u>opened</u> [unlocked] the door to the cage. The monkeys <u>left</u> [escaped]. The zookeeper <u>looked</u> [searched] everywhere for the monkeys. The monkeys <u>ran</u> [raced] through the park. They <u>had</u> [ate] hot dogs, peanuts, and popcorn. Then they <u>went back</u> [returned] to their cage. The monkeys <u>will rest</u> [will sleep] after their exciting day.

Score: _____   Total Possible: 16

122

D. Complete each sentence by filling in the five blank spaces with adjectives. Sample answers are given.

The baby birds waited patiently in their ___warm___ [1] nest. The nest was safe in a ___pine___ [2] tree. Soon the mother bird returned to feed her ___hungry___ [3] babies. The mother bird carried a ___wiggly___ [4] worm in her beak. ___Five___ [5] baby birds and only one worm. What should she do?

Score: _____   Total Possible: 5

E. Underline the nine adverbs in the paragraph below.

The sky darkened <u>slowly</u> all afternoon. <u>Finally</u>, it began to snow. The flakes drifted <u>lazily</u> over the grass and trees. The ground was <u>soon</u> covered with a soft, white blanket. The wind <u>suddenly</u> shifted, and the storm <u>quickly</u> began. The wind roared <u>loudly</u> through the tree branches. The snow <u>swiftly</u> piled against the windows. Within an hour, it was <u>almost</u> a foot deep.

Score: _____   Total Possible: 9

F. Choose the article (a, an, the) that best completes each sentence. Write it on the line. Sample answers are given.

"To live long, live hidden" is the motto of many animals. For some animals, ___the___ [1] best defense is to hold completely still so that their predators won't notice them. Some animals are protected by ___a___ [2] change in color that can make them almost invisible. In polar areas, ___a___ [3] creature might have fur that turns white to blend in with ___the___ [4] snow. Spots and stripes can help other animals hide in ___an___ [5] area with tall grass or leaves.

Score: _____   Total Possible: 5

REVIEW SCORE: _____   REVIEW TOTAL: 58

123

Lesson 60

Lesson 60 Grammar: Statements and Questions I

Do you know that there are different kinds of sentences? A good writer knows exactly when to use each kind.

.... **Did You Know?** ....

A sentence can be a statement or a question.
A <u>statement</u> is a sentence that gives information. It ends with a period (.).
  Dalmatians are large dogs with black spots**.**
  They do not have spots when they are born**.**
A <u>question</u> is a sentence that asks for information. It ends with a question mark (?).
  How are dalmatian puppies different from adults**?**
  What do dalmatians look like**?**

....

Show What You Know

Add a period or a question mark at the end of each of the sentences in the paragraph.

What scared the impala**?** It was a leopard that leaped out of the bush**.** Leopards hunt other animals by sneaking up on them**.** They eat reptiles and small mammals**.** Leopards do not have very many enemies**.** Baboons, lions, and hyenas will attack baby leopards**.** Who is the leopard's greatest enemy**?** It is the people who hunt leopards for their beautiful coats**.**

Score: _____   Total Possible: 8

124

Practice

Write two sentences that give information.

1. _____
Review sentences to be sure your child has:
  • written sentences that are grammatically correct.
  • written sentences that are statements.
2. _____
  • used periods correctly.

_____

Revise

Now, make questions from the statements you wrote above. You can use words like *who, what, where, when, why,* or *how* to make questions.

1. _____
Review sentences to be sure your child has:
  • written sentences that are grammatically correct.
2. _____
  • written sentences that are questions.
  • used question marks correctly.

Tips for Your Own Writing: Revising ....

When you are checking your writing, look for sentences that begin with such words as *who, what, where, when, why,* and *how.* These words often begin questions. Be sure you placed a question mark at the end of sentences that begin with these words and ask a question.

In sentences that ask, use a question mark; in sentences that tell, use a period.

125

Lesson 61

Lesson

61 Grammar: Statements and Questions II

Statements tell and questions ask.

.... **Did You Know?** ....

Some sentences tell facts and others ask questions. Each kind of sentence has its own job to do. Each kind of sentence uses a different end mark.

A sentence that gives information is a **statement** and ends with a **period**.

> Most deserts get fewer than ten inches of rain in a year**.**

A sentence that asks for information is a **question** and ends with a **question mark**.

> How much rain do most deserts get in a year**?**

....

Show What You Know

Add a period at the end of each sentence that is a statement. Add a question mark to the end of each sentence that asks for information.

Where do the President and his family live?The President's home is at 1600 Pennsylvania Avenue.Have you ever heard of the White House Gang? They were the six children of President Theodore Roosevelt.They had lots of fun when they lived in the White House.They roller-skated in the halls, slid on trays down the stairs, and walked on stilts in the flower gardens.They had many pets: dogs, cats, rabbits, birds, and a pony.Once they brought their pony upstairs in an elevator.What do you think President Roosevelt said when the elevator door opened?Who would have believed there was a pony on the elevator?

Score: _____ Total Possible: 10

126

Practice

Your home is not as famous as the White House, but there are probably lots of interesting facts about it. Make a list of facts about your home. Use statements in your list.

Review the list to make sure your child

has used the correct punctuation

for a statement.

Revise

Now, pretend that you are giving a friend a tour of your home. Write a conversation that you and your friend might have. Use your list of facts to write questions and statements.

Review sentences to make sure your child has added the correct punctuation.

Tips for Your Own Writing: Revising ....

Choose a piece of your own writing. Underline sentences that ask for information. Check to make sure that each underlined sentence ends with a question mark.

Ask me a question, and I will answer in a statement.

127

....

Lesson 62

Lesson

62 Grammar: Exclamations

In writing, to say it with feeling, use an exclamation point.

.... **Did You Know?** ....

A sentence that expresses strong feeling is an **exclamatory** sentence. It ends with an exclamation point.

> It was so hot!
> Look at the beautiful sunset!
> Be careful!

When you are reading, end punctuation marks tell you what tone of voice you would use if you were speaking. In this way, periods, question marks, and exclamation points are signposts for the reader.

Read the sentences aloud. Notice how your voice changes as you read each one.

> I'm hungry!
> Where are we going?
> Nick ate cereal and fruit for breakfast.

....

Show What You Know

After each sentence, add the correct punctuation.

A little green man was sitting at the table when I got home from school.He said that his name was Zornak and that he came from outer space.He had eaten all the food in the kitchen.Boy, Mom's going to be mad about that!I heard steps on the porch.Where should I hide him?"Hurry, get in the closet!" My little brother Eddie came into the room.Could I trust him with my secret? Here goes nothing!I opened the closet door."Eddie, meet Zornak," I said.

Score: _____ Total Possible: 12

128

Practice

Pretend you came home from school and found something unexpected in your house. Write a paragraph that tells about what you found and how you reacted.

Check sentences to make sure your child has:

• written complete sentences.

• used appropriate end punctuation.

• written sentences that respond to the prompt and stay on the topic.

Revise

Review your paragraph. Rewrite two sentences to show strong feelings. Be sure to end those sentences with exclamation points.

Review sentences to make sure your child has:

• revised two sentences.

• formed exclamatory sentences.

Tips for Your Own Writing: Revising ....

You use an exclamation point at the end of a sentence to show strong feelings. Using too many exclamation points weakens their meaning. Not everything is exciting. Check your writing. If you have used more than two or three exclamation points, you may want to change some of them to periods.

When feelings are strong, exclamation points belong!

129

Lesson 63

Lesson 63 Grammar: Statements, Questions, and Exclamations

✎ "*Have I used the correct punctuation?" is an important question to ask.*

.... Did You Know? ....

Writers use different kinds of sentences.
Most sentences will be statements.
Uncle Jon likes to barbecue.
Some will ask questions.
Does he cook outside often?
A few sentences will express strong feelings, like excitement, anger, surprise, or fear. This kind of sentence ends with an exclamation point (!).
His smoked chicken is out-of-this-world!

Show What You Know
Add correct punctuation to the end of each sentence in the paragraph.

It is a hot, sunny day in southern Florida. Do you see an area of swirling clouds off the coast? Wind speeds are more than 100 miles per hour! Weather reporters name this storm Hurricane Barbara. The storm is strong enough to rip trees out of the ground. The giant, spinning mass of clouds gains speed over the water. The winds shape the clouds into an enormous doughnut. Will it move west to the coast, or will it head out to sea? Sometimes computers can predict the path of a storm. Other times, the hurricane has a mind of its own!

Score: _____   Total Possible: 10

130

Practice
Choose one of the questions from the list below. Write two statements that answer the question.

Should my school require students to wear uniforms?
Is a cat a better pet than a dog?
Do you like the Fourth of July? Why or why not?

1. _____ Review sentences to be sure your child has:

    • written sentences to support the topic.

2. _____ • written statements.

    • used end punctuation correctly.

Revise
Review the sentences you have written. Now change your statements into questions, but not the same questions as those given above. Make sure you use question marks at the end of your questions.

1. _____ Review sentences to be sure your child:

    • written questions.

2. _____ • used end punctuation correctly.

Tips for Your Own Writing: Revising ....
Most of the sentences you write will be statements. Check to make sure they end with periods. When you do ask questions, always end the sentences with question marks. To show strong feelings, you can end your sentences with an exclamation point.

✎ *When a sentence tells, a period is swell. For a question, it's true that a question mark will do.*

131

Lesson 64

Lesson 64 Review: Sentence Types

A. Use proper proofreading marks to add a period or question mark at the end of each of the ten sentences.

Koalas are small, furry animals that live in Australia. Why did the aborigines call these mammals koalas? Koala means "one who doesn't drink." How do koalas get the water they need? They eat tender eucalyptus leaves that are almost two-thirds water. No other animal in the forest eats eucalyptus. The koalas spend most of their lives high in the eucalyptus trees. Do they ever come down? They come down to move to another tree to find more food. A koala eats about two pounds of leaves a day.

Score: _____   Total Possible: 10

B. Here is part of a story. The writer forgot to use end marks. Use proper proofreading marks to add periods and question marks to these twelve sentences.

We have been in the desert for two days. The midday sun shimmers on the hot sand. We are almost out of water. Are my eyes playing tricks on me? Sometimes people think they see water in the desert. Right over the next dune, I see a cool, blue pool of water surrounded by lush, green trees. Is that a camel? Is he sitting on a lawn chair sipping a glass of lemonade? I run toward the oasis. I feel someone tapping on my arm. I wake up from my nap at the pool and see my sister. She says, "How about a nice, cool drink?"

Score: _____   Total Possible: 12

132

C. Only periods were used in this paragraph. Use proofreading marks to revise three sentences by changing one period to a question mark and two periods to exclamation points.

Imagine living in the age of the dinosaurs. What do you think you would see? The area around you would be filled with unfamiliar plants and trees. You would see some peaceful, plant-eating animals. You might run into some fierce, flesh-eating killers, too! A brachiosaurus was as long as three school buses and as tall as a five-story building. It could have weighed as much as sixteen elephants. Others were as small as a chicken. Ornithopods were little, but they could sprint as fast as a galloping horse!

Score: _____   Total Possible: 3

D. Choose one group of words from Column A and one from Column B to make sentences. Make two statements, one question, and one exclamatory sentence using the correct end marks.

Column A	Column B
We live in a galaxy	a shooting star
How many	around 500,000 million stars in our galaxy
There are	called the Milky Way
Look! I see	stars are in our galaxy

We live in a galaxy called the Milky Way.

How many stars are in our galaxy?

There are around 500,000 million stars in our galaxy.

Look! I see a shooting star!

Score: _____   Total Possible: 4

REVIEW SCORE: _____   REVIEW TOTAL: 29

133

Lesson 65

Lesson

65 Grammar: Understanding Sentences I

Writing a sentence is easy if you tell who or what did what.

.... **Did You Know?** ....

A *sentence* tells *who* or *what*, and it tells *what happens.*

My dog Buster   won first prize.
(tells who)   (tells what happened)

....

Show What You Know
Underline the groups of words that are sentences.

1. <u>Harry lives in a cage.</u>
2. A small, chunky hamster.
3. <u>He has a short tail and chubby cheeks.</u>
4. <u>His fur is reddish-brown.</u>
5. The pouches in his cheeks.
6. Sleeps all day.
7. <u>Fruit, grains, and raw vegetables make up Harry's diet.</u>
8. <u>He runs on a little wheel.</u>
9. In his cage.
10. Lots of fun.

Score: _____   Total Possible: 5

134

Practice
Make the sentences below complete. For some sentences, you must add words that tell who or what. For other sentences, you must add words that tell what happened.
Sample answers are given.

1. The girls _____liked to visit their grandmother_____
2. _____Grandma_____ lived near Boulder, Colorado.
3. Her house _____was built on a huge hill_____
4. _____My kitten_____ wears glasses.

Revise
Read the paragraph. Underline the three incomplete sentences. Add words that tell who, what, or what happened and write the corrected sentences on the lines.
Sample answers are given.

Our apartment has only two bedrooms. <u>My two little brothers and I.</u> John and Matt are lucky. <u>Get to sleep in bunk beds.</u> I sleep in a bed on the other side of the room. Sometimes, I wish I had my own room. <u>Then my friends and I.</u> Sometimes, I like sharing a room. We all have to clean it even when only I made the mess.

_____My two little brothers and I share a room._____

_____My brothers get to sleep in bunk beds._____

_____Then my friends and I wouldn't have my little brothers in our way._____

Tips for Your Own Writing: Revising ....
When checking a sentence you have written, ask yourself: Does my sentence tell who, what, or what happened? If your answer is *no*, then you must revise your sentence until you can answer *yes*.

A sentence won't work if it's missing parts!

135

....

Lesson 66

Lesson

66 Grammar: Understanding Sentences II

Reading short, choppy sentences can be boring. Once you get your readers started, help them keep rolling. Sometimes putting sentences together can make your writing flow more smoothly.

.... **Did You Know?** ....

Sometimes two sentences have ideas that are equally important. They can be joined to make one sentence using a comma and the word *and.*

Springfield is the capital of Illinois.
Madison is the capital of Wisconsin.
Springfield is the capital of Illinois, **and** Madison is the capital of Wisconsin.

If the ideas in two sentences seem opposed to each other, use a comma and the word *but* to join them.

My dog is really ugly.   I love him anyway.
My dog is really ugly, **but** I love him anyway.

If there is a choice in the two sentences, use a comma and the word *or* to join them.

We can visit the aquarium. We can go to the zoo instead.
We can visit the aquarium, **or** we can go to the zoo instead.

....

Show What You Know
Choose *and*, *or*, or *but* to join each set of sentences. Write the new sentences. Do not forget to add a comma before *and*, *but*, or *or*.

Mary is my older sister. Megan is my younger sister.

1. _____Mary is my older sister, and Megan is my younger sister._____

We get along pretty well. Sometimes we fight over using the telephone.

2. _____We get along pretty well, but sometimes we fight over using the telephone._____

Score: _____   Total Possible: 2

136

Practice
Look at the picture. Write two sentences to describe what is happening using *and*, *or*, or *but*.

_____Review the sentences to be sure your child has:_____

_____• written compound sentences._____

_____• placed a comma before the conjunction._____

Revise
Read the following paragraph. Use proofreading marks to add *and*, *but*, or *or* to combine four sentences that you think should go together. Remember to place a comma before *and*, *but*, or *or*.

Example: I like to collect baseball cards. My sister doesn't.

Do you like to collect sports cards? My sister and I do. I collect baseball cards. My sister collects basketball cards. I keep my cards in a shoe box. My sister organizes all her cards in a photo album. My older brother used to collect baseball cards, too. He doesn't anymore. Maybe he will give his cards to me. Maybe he will sell them. I hope he gives them to me.

Review the sentences to be sure your child has combined sentences appropriately; used *and*, *but*, and *or*; and added a comma before each *and*, *but*, or *or*.

Tips for Your Own Writing: Revising ....
Sometimes you may write short sentences that can be combined. Check that you place a comma before the *and*, *but*, or *or* when you combine them. Make sure you use *and* to connect sentences with similar ideas, use *but* to connect sentences with opposing ideas, and use *or* to connect sentences that give choices.

*If combining sentences is what you want to do, a comma and *and*, *but*, or *or* can always help you.*

137

Lesson 67

<table>
<tr><td>

Lesson

67 Grammar: Combining Sentences I

*W*hen two people or things do the same thing, try to tell about it in one sentence when you can.

.... **Did You Know?** ....

To combine sentences that have some of the words repeated, use the repeated words only once and the word *and* to join the sentences. Remember to change the verb form to agree with the plural subject.

Maria likes to hike in the mountains.
Tanya likes to hike in the mountains.
Maria and Tanya like to hike in the mountains.

If you use *I* as part of a combined subject, do not forget to put *I* last.

I am going to summer camp.
Keith is going to summer camp.
Keith and I are going to summer camp.

Show What You Know

Combine each set of sentences below to form one sentence. Use *and* to connect two nouns or pronouns.

1. My grandpa collects stamps. I collect stamps.

   My grandpa and I collect stamps.

2. My sister sometimes gives me stamps. My dad sometimes gives me stamps.

   My sister and my dad sometimes give me stamps.

3. Rare stamps are valuable. Stamps with printing errors are valuable.

   Rare stamps and stamps with printing errors are valuable.

Score: _____   Total Possible: 3

138

</td><td>

Practice

On another piece of paper, make a Venn diagram like the one below to show how one of your hobbies and a classmate's hobby are the same.

My Hobby	Both are collections.	Classmate's Hobby
model airplane my father started my collection		model car my grandma started my collection

Write two sentences telling about how your hobbies are the same.

Review the sentences to be sure your child has:

• expressed a complete thought in each sentence.

• written about how both hobbies are the same.

• used *and* to connect nouns and pronouns.

• placed the word *I* last in a combined subject.

Revise

Rewrite each pair of sentences below to form one sentence.

1. Peas never stay on your fork. Meatballs never stay on your fork.

   Peas and meatballs never stay on your fork.

2. Lemons will make you pucker. Sour grapes will make you pucker.

   Lemons and sour grapes will make you pucker.

Tips for Your Own Writing: Revising ....

Remember that you must change the verb to agree with a combined subject. Also be sure to place the pronoun *I* last if you combine it with another pronoun or a noun as part of a subject.

*T*o combine subjects, the rules are these: subject and verb must agree, and *I* goes last in order to please.

139

</td></tr>
</table>

Lesson 68

<table>
<tr><td>

Lesson

68 Grammar: Combining Sentences II

*I*f you have one person doing more than one thing, then place the verbs in a string.

.... **Did You Know?** ....

A good writer can combine sentences in several ways. One way is to combine two sentences that have some of the words repeated. Use the repeated words only once, and use *and* or *or* to join the sentences.

Gloria washed the dishes. Gloria dried the dishes.
Gloria washed **and** dried the dishes.

Gloria could dust the furniture. Gloria could vacuum the carpet.
Gloria could dust the furniture **or** vacuum the carpet.

Show What You Know

Combine each pair of sentences below into one sentence that has two verbs, or action words.

1. Helen Keller could not see. Helen Keller could not hear.

   Helen Keller could not see or hear.

2. Helen could read Braille. Helen could write on a special typewriter.

   Helen could read Braille and write on a special typewriter.

3. She went to high school. She graduated from Radcliffe College.

   She went to high school and graduated from Radcliffe College.

4. Helen wrote books. Helen received many honors for helping others.

   Helen wrote books and received many honors for helping others.

Score: _____   Total Possible: 4

140

</td><td>

Practice

Think about a person who interests you. Write down action words that you might use to tell about the person (wrote, published, invented). Then write two short sentences with compound action verbs about the person.

Review the sentences to be sure your child has:

• used the words *and* or *or* to combine verbs in a

sentence.

• not repeated the subject.

Revise

Combine each pair of sentences below by using repeated words only once. Use the word *and* to connect the verbs and their objects in the sentences.

1. Frédéric Bartholdi, from France, built a giant metal statue. Frédéric Bartholdi called it the Statue of Liberty.

   Frédéric Bartholdi, from France, built a giant metal statue and called it the Statue of Liberty.

2. The statue was built so that people can climb up inside. People look out through the crown.

   The statue was built so that people can climb up inside and look out through the crown.

Tips for Your Own Writing: Revising ....

Find a piece of your own writing. Look for two sentences that tell about the same person, place, thing, or idea. If you find any, combine them into one.

*O*ne subject and two verbs can be combined to make your sentences more refined.

141

</td></tr>
</table>

Lesson 69

Lesson
69 Grammar: Combining Sentences III

✏️ *If readers you want to win, avoid writing sentences that repeat the same words again and again.*

.... Did You Know? ....

A good writer can combine sentences in several ways. One way is to use *and* **to combine sentences that have some of the words repeated so that the repeated words are used only once.**

Kenji likes apples. Kenji likes oranges.
Kenji likes apples **and** oranges.

If more than two things are named, put a comma after each one, and add *and* **before the last one.**

Veronica has a dog. Veronica has a cat. Veronica has two goldfish.
Veronica has a dog, a cat, **and** two goldfish.

....

Show What You Know
Combine each set of sentences below into one sentence.

1. Our class took a trip to New York City. Our class took a trip to Washington, D.C.

   Our class took a trip to New York City and Washington, D.C.

2. We traveled by plane. We traveled by train. We traveled by bus.

   We traveled by plane, train, and bus.

3. We saw the Empire State Building. We saw the World Trade Center. We saw the Washington Monument.

   We saw the Empire State Building, the World Trade Center, and the Washington Monument.

Score: _____   Total Possible: 3

142

Practice
Look at the picture. Write two sentences with compound parts to describe what you see. Keep your sentences short and to the point.

1. _____ Review sentences to be sure your child has:

   • written sentences that reflect the activities pictured.

   • written sentences with *and* to combine

2. _____ compound parts.

   • used commas to separate items if they name more than two things.

Revise
Combine the following sets of sentences to avoid repeating words.

1. Elephants eat leaves. Elephants eat grass and fruit.

   Elephants eat leaves, grass, and fruit.

2. The African elephant has four toenails on its front feet. The African elephant has three toenails on its back feet.

   The African elephant has four toenails on its front feet and three toenails on its back feet.

3. Today, many African and Asian countries protect the elephants. Today many African and Asian nations protect their habitats.

   Today, many African and Asian countries protect the elephants and their habitats.

Tips for Your Own Writing: Revising ....
When you combine more than two items in a sentence, make sure you place a comma after each item except the last one. Write the word *and* before the last item listed.

✏️ *One subject and one verb can stand with many words when you use* and.

143

· ·

Lesson 70

Lesson
70 Grammar: Combining Sentences IV

✏️ *Sometimes one sentence will do in place of two.*

.... Did You Know? ....

Sometimes you can improve your writing by using one or two words in place of a whole sentence.

Grandma baked muffins. They were delicious.
Grandma baked **delicious** muffins.

You can often combine basic information from several sentences into one sentence.

Grandma has a garden. It is in the backyard. It is big.
Grandma has a **big** garden **in the backyard** *or*
Grandma has a **big, backyard** garden.

....

Show What You Know
Combine each group of sentences below into one sentence.

1. Rosa is going on a trip. She is going to Dallas. The trip is short.

   Rosa is going on a short trip to Dallas.

2. She packs a suitcase. It is brown. It is big.

   She packs a big, brown suitcase.

3. Uncle Larry carries the suitcase to the car. The suitcase is heavy.

   Uncle Larry carries the heavy suitcase to the car.

4. Doug meets Rosa at the airport. Rosa is Doug's cousin.

   Doug meets his cousin Rosa at the airport.

Score: _____   Total Possible: 4

144

Practice
Look at the picture and write two sentences with two adjectives connected by *and* **to tell what the lucky pirate found.**

1. _____ Review sentences to be sure your child has:

   • described what is happening in the picture.

   • written sentences with compound adjectives.

2. _____ • used commas correctly.

Revise
Combine the following pairs of sentences. Write your sentences on the lines.

1. A sheepdog has long hair. Its shaggy hair covers its eyes.

   A sheepdog has long, shaggy hair that covers its eyes.

2. A dachshund's legs are short. Its stumpy legs are powerful.

   A dachshund's short, stumpy legs are powerful.

3. The Chihuahua has bulging eyes. The eyes are very large.

   The Chihuahua has very large, bulging eyes.

Tips for Your Own Writing: Revising ....
When you are proofreading sentences you have combined, make sure that you have not added adjectives that have the same or similar meanings.

✏️ *When possible, replace a sentence with a word or two to make your writing more efficient.*

145

Lesson 71

Lesson 71 — Grammar: Combining Sentences V

Using phrases in sentences lets you say more—with less!

.... Did You Know? ....

In writing, you can combine short sentences to save space and add variety. Sometimes you can improve your writing by using a phrase in place of a whole sentence.

My birthday present was a CD player. It was from Mom and Dad.

My birthday present **from Mom and Dad** was a CD player.

Show What You Know

Combine each pair of sentences into one sentence. Use a phrase in place of one sentence. Sample answers are given.

1. Oscar went sailing. He went with Ramon.

   Oscar went sailing with Ramon.

2. They sailed east. They left from the harbor.

   They sailed east from the harbor.

3. Oscar had supplies. He stored them beneath the deck.

   Oscar stored supplies beneath the deck.

4. They docked the boat. The dock was past the cove.

   They docked the boat past the cove.

5. Oscar and Ramon had a picnic. They sat near some rocks.

   Oscar and Ramon had a picnic near some rocks.

Score: _____   Total Possible: 5

146

Practice

Write a poem by adding nouns, verbs, and other words to the following phrases. Sample answers are given.

There was an old cat sleeping ___ in the house.

It was awakened ___ by a mouse.

It chased the mouse ___ across the floor.

The mouse jumped and ran ___ out the door.

Review the poem to be sure your child has added nouns and verbs to the phrases.

Revise

In the paragraph below, combine sentences by using phrases. Write your new sentences on the lines.

Mars is the fourth planet from the sun. Mars is in our solar system. Mars looks red because iron oxide is in the soil. Iron oxide is also in the rocks. Mars is the only planet with ice caps besides Earth. The ice caps are located at the poles.

Mars is the fourth planet from the sun in our solar system.

Mars looks red because iron oxide is in the soil and also in the rocks. Mars is the only planet with ice caps at the poles besides Earth.

Tips for Your Own Writing: Revising ....

You can use words like *above, across, before, during, from, in, into, on, over, under,* and *with* to begin a phrase when revising your writing.

"During the nights and the days" is an example of a phrase.

147

Lesson 72

Lesson 72 — Review: Sentences

A. Add the missing words to complete each of the seven sentences. Sample answers are given.

The animals who live in Animalville lead a different life from most other animals. In the morning, they __meet and have breakfast__[1] . __Then they go to the park__[2] to have a picnic lunch. Sometimes the baby monkeys __play on the swing set__[3] . __Some of them decorate__[4] the trees with balloons and streamers. The baby tigers __chase their tails__[5] . __They like to__[6] make the other animals laugh. All of the animals __have a good time__[7] .

Score: _____   Total Possible: 7

B. Combine each pair of sentences below into one compound sentence. You may want to use *and, but,* or *or* to connect the sentences. Sample answers are given.

1. Brian and Karen went to the video store. They looked for a movie.

   Brian and Karen went to the video store, and they looked for a movie.

2. Karen wanted to rent *Babe*. Brian had already seen it.

   Karen wanted to rent *Babe*, but Brian had already seen it.

3. Brian decided to get *The Indian in the Cupboard*. Karen liked his choice.

   Brian decided to get *The Indian in the Cupboard*, and Karen liked his choice.

4. They have to return the movie tomorrow. The video store will charge a $2 late fee.

   They have to return the movie tomorrow, or the video store will charge a $2 late fee.

Score: _____   Total Possible: 4

148

C. Combine the following sentences by making the subjects, verbs, or objects compound.

1. Hidori helped Dad plan a trip. Lee helped Dad plan a trip.

   Hidori and Lee helped Dad plan a trip.

2. In the car, Hidori read. Hidori listened to the radio.

   In the car, Hidori read and listened to the radio.

3. They visited a zoo. They visited a planetarium. They visited a museum.

   They visited a zoo, a planetarium, and a museum.

Score: _____   Total Possible: 3

D. Combine each set of sentences into one sentence.

1. Kangaroos are furry mammals. They are unusual.

   Kangaroos are unusual, furry mammals.

2. Kangaroos hop on their powerful hind legs. Their legs are long.

   Kangaroos hop on their long, powerful hind legs.

Score: _____   Total Possible: 2

E. Combine each pair of sentences into one sentence. Use a phrase in place of a sentence.

1. Bears are big and powerful animals. They are animals with long, thick fur.

   Bears are big and powerful animals with long, thick fur.

2. Bear cubs live with their mother. They stay with her for about one or two years.

   Bear cubs live with their mother for about one or two years.

Score: _____   Total Possible: 2

REVIEW SCORE: _____   REVIEW TOTAL: 18

149

Proofreading Marks

lowercase: / $\cancel{S}$ister

capitalize: ≡ o̲h̲io

delete: ℓ w̶o̶r̶dℓ

transpose: ∿ sheep⸝s⸜ wool

insert: ∧   beautiful
     a ∧ sunset

add...   a comma: ⌄

     a period: ⊙

     a colon: ⋏

     a semicolon: ⋏

     a quotation mark: ＂ⱽ

     an apostrophe: ⱽ

McGraw-Hill Consumer Products

The skills taught in school are now available at home!
These award-winning software titles meet school guidelines and are based on
The McGraw-Hill Companies classroom software titles.

MATH GRADES 1 & 2

These math programs are a great way to teach and reinforce skills used in everyday situations. Fun, friendly characters need help with their math skills. Everyone's friend, Nubby the stubby pencil, will help kids master the math in the Numbers Quiz show. Foggy McHammer, a carpenter, needs some help building his playhouse so that all the boards will fit together! Julio Bambino's kitchen antics will surely burn his pastries if you don't help him set the clock timer correctly! We can't forget Turbo Tomato, a fruit with a passion for adventure, who needs help calculating his daredevil stunts.

Math Grades 1 & 2 use a tested, proven approach to reinforcing your child's math skills while keeping him or her intrigued with Nubby and his collection of crazy friends.

TITLE	ISBN	PRICE
Grade 1: Nubby's Quiz Show	1-57768-321-8	$9.95
Grade 2: Foggy McHammer's Treehouse	1-57768-322-6	$9.95

Available in jewel case only (no box included)

MISSION MASTERS™ MATH AND LANGUAGE ARTS

The Mission Masters™—Pauline, Rakeem, Mia, and T.J.—need your help. The Mission Masters™ are a team of young agents working for the Intelliforce Agency, a high-level cooperative whose goal is to maintain order on our rather unruly planet. From within the agency's top secret Command Control Center, the agency's central computer, M5, has detected a threat...and guess what—you're the agent assigned to the mission!

MISSION MASTERS™ MATH GRADES 3, 4, & 5

This series of exciting activities encourages young mathematicians to challenge themselves and their math skills to overcome the perils of villains and other planetary threats. Skills reinforced include: analyzing and solving real-world problems, estimation, measurements, geometry, whole numbers, fractions, graphs, and patterns.

TITLE	ISBN	PRICE
Grade 3: Mission Masters™ Defeat Dirty D!	1-57768-323-5	$9.95
Grade 4: Mission Masters™ Alien Encounter	1-57768-324-2	$9.95
Grade 5: Mission Masters™ Meet Mudflat Moe	1-57768-325-0	$9.95

Available in jewel case only (no box included)

MISSION MASTERS™ LANGUAGE ARTS GRADES 3, 4, & 5

This series invites children to apply their language skills to defeat unscrupulous characters and to overcome other earthly dangers. Skills reinforced include: language mechanics and usage, punctuation, spelling, vocabulary, reading comprehension, and creative writing.

TITLE	ISBN	PRICE
Grade 3: Mission Masters™ Freezing Frenzy	1-57768-343-9	$9.95
Grade 4: Mission Masters™ Network Nightmare	1-57768-344-7	$9.95
Grade 5: Mission Masters™ Mummy Mysteries	1-57768-345-5	$9.95

Available in jewel case only (no box included)

BASIC SKILLS BUILDER K to 2 – THE MAGIC APPLEHOUSE

At the Magic Applehouse, children discover that Abigail Appleseed runs a deliciously successful business selling apple pies, tarts, and other apple treats. Enthusiasm grows as children join in the fun of helping Abigail run her business. Along the way they'll develop computer and entrepreneurial skills to last a lifetime. They will run their own business – all while they're having bushels of fun!

TITLE	ISBN	PRICE
Basic Skills Builder –The Magic Applehouse	1-57768-312-9	$9.95

Available in jewel case only (no box included)

TEST PREP – SCORING HIGH

This grade-based testing software will help prepare your child for standardized achievement tests given by his or her school. Scoring High specifically targets the skills required for success on the Stanford Achievement Test (SAT) for grades three through eight. Lessons and test questions follow the same format and cover the same content areas as questions appearing on the actual SAT tests. The practice tests are modeled after the SAT test-taking experience with similar directions, number of questions per section, and bubble-sheet answer choices.

Scoring High is a child's first-class ticket to a winning score on standardized achievement tests!

TITLE	ISBN	PRICE
Grades 3 to 5: Scoring High Test Prep	1-57768-316-1	$9.95
Grades 6 to 8: Scoring High Test Prep	1-57768-317-X	$9.95

Available in jewel case only (no box included)

SCIENCE

Mastering the principles of both physical and life science has never been so FUN for kids grades six and above as it is while they are exploring McGraw-Hill's edutainment software!

TITLE	ISBN	PRICE
Grades 6 & up: Life Science	1-57768-336-6	$9.95
Grades 8 & up: Physical Science	1-57768-308-0	$9.95

Available in jewel case only (no box included)

REFERENCE

The National Museum of Women in the Arts has teamed with McGraw-Hill Consumer Products to bring you this superb collection available for your enjoyment on CD-ROM.

This special collection is a visual diary of 200 women artists from the Renaissance to the present, spanning 500 years of creativity.

You will discover the art of women who excelled in all the great art movements of history. Artists who pushed the boundaries of abstract, genre, landscape, narrative, portrait, and still-life styles; as well as artists forced to push the societal limits placed on women through the ages.

TITLE	ISBN	PRICE
Women in the Arts	1-57768-010-3	$29.95

Available in boxed version only

Most titles for Windows 3.1™, Windows '95™ & '98™, and Macintosh™.

Visit us on the Internet at:

www.MHkids.com

Or call 800-298-4119 for your local retailer.

All our workbooks meet school curriculum guidelines and correspond to The McGraw-Hill Companies classroom textbooks.

SPECTRUM SERIES

DOLCH Sight Word Activities

The DOLCH Sight Word Activities Workbooks use the classic Dolch list of 220 basic vocabulary words that make up from 50% to 75% of all reading matter that children ordinarily encounter. Since these words are ordinarily recognized on sight, they are called *sight words*. Volume 1 includes 110 sight words. Volume 2 covers the remainder of the list. Over 160 pages.

TITLE	ISBN	PRICE
Grades K-1 Vol. 1	1-57768-429-X	$9.95
Grades K-1 Vol. 2	1-57768-439-7	$9.95

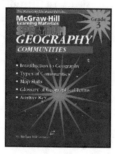

GEOGRAPHY

Full-color, three-part lessons strengthen geography knowledge and map reading skills. Focusing on five geographic themes including location, place, human/environmental interaction, movement, and regions. Over 150 pages. Glossary of geographical terms and answer key included.

TITLE	ISBN	PRICE
Gr 3, Communities	1-57768-153-3	$7.95
Gr 4, Regions	1-57768-154-1	$7.95
Gr 5, USA	1-57768-155-X	$7.95
Gr 6, World	1-57768-156-8	$7.95

MATH

Features easy-to-follow instructions that give students a clear path to success. This series has comprehensive coverage of the basic skills, helping children to master math fundamentals. Over 150 pages. Answer key included.

TITLE	ISBN	PRICE
Grade 1	1-57768-111-8	$7.95
Grade 2	1-57768-112-6	$7.95
Grade 3	1-57768-113-4	$7.95
Grade 4	1-57768-114-2	$7.95
Grade 5	1-57768-115-0	$7.95
Grade 6	1-57768-116-9	$7.95
Grade 7	1-57768-117-7	$7.95
Grade 8	1-57768-118-5	$7.95

PHONICS

Provides everything children need to build multiple skills in language. Focusing on phonics, structural analysis, and dictionary skills, this series also offers creative ideas for using phonics and word study skills in other language arts. Over 200 pages. Answer key included.

TITLE	ISBN	PRICE
Grade K	1-57768-120-7	$7.95
Grade 1	1-57768-121-5	$7.95
Grade 2	1-57768-122-3	$7.95
Grade 3	1-57768-123-1	$7.95
Grade 4	1-57768-124-X	$7.95
Grade 5	1-57768-125-8	$7.95
Grade 6	1-57768-126-6	$7.95

READING

This full-color series creates an enjoyable reading environment, even for below-average readers. Each book contains captivating content, colorful characters, and compelling illustrations, so children are eager to find out what happens next. Over 150 pages. Answer key included.

TITLE	ISBN	PRICE
Grade K	1-57768-130-4	$7.95
Grade 1	1-57768-131-2	$7.95
Grade 2	1-57768-132-0	$7.95
Grade 3	1-57768-133-9	$7.95
Grade 4	1-57768-134-7	$7.95
Grade 5	1-57768-135-5	$7.95
Grade 6	1-57768-136-3	$7.95

SPELLING

This full-color series links spelling to reading and writing and increases skills in words and meanings, consonant and vowel spellings, and proofreading practice. Over 200 pages. Speller dictionary and answer key included.

TITLE	ISBN	PRICE
Grade 1	1-57768-161-4	$7.95
Grade 2	1-57768-162-2	$7.95
Grade 3	1-57768-163-0	$7.95
Grade 4	1-57768-164-9	$7.95
Grade 5	1-57768-165-7	$7.95
Grade 6	1-57768-166-5	$7.95

WRITING

Lessons focus on creative and expository writing using clearly stated objectives and pre-writing exercises. Eight essential reading skills are applied. Activities include main idea, sequence, comparison, detail, fact and opinion, cause and effect, and making a point. Over 130 pages. Answer key included.

TITLE	ISBN	PRICE
Grade 1	1-57768-141-X	$7.95
Grade 2	1-57768-142-8	$7.95
Grade 3	1-57768-143-6	$7.95
Grade 4	1-57768-144-4	$7.95
Grade 5	1-57768-145-2	$7.95
Grade 6	1-57768-146-0	$7.95
Grade 7	1-57768-147-9	$7.95
Grade 8	1-57768-148-7	$7.95

TEST PREP
From the Nation's #1 Testing Company

Prepares children to do their best on current editions of the five major standardized tests. Activities reinforce test-taking skills through examples, tips, practice, and timed exercises. Subjects include reading, math, and language. Over 150 pages. Answer key included.

TITLE	ISBN	PRICE
Grade 1	1-57768-101-0	$8.95
Grade 2	1-57768-102-9	$8.95
Grade 3	1-57768-103-7	$8.95
Grade 4	1-57768-104-5	$8.95
Grade 5	1-57768-105-3	$8.95
Grade 6	1-57768-106-1	$8.95
Grade 7	1-57768-107-X	$8.95
Grade 8	1-57768-108-8	$8.95

LANGUAGE ARTS

Encourages creativity and builds confidence by making writing fun! Seventy-two four-part lessons strengthen writing skills by focusing on parts of speech, word usage, sentence structure, punctuation, and proofreading. Each level includes a *Writer's Handbook* at the end of the book that offers writing tips. This series is based on the highly respected SRA/McGraw-Hill language arts series. More than 180 full-color pages. *Available March 2000.*

TITLE	ISBN	PRICE
Grade 2	1-57768-472-9	$7.95
Grade 3	1-57768-473-7	$7.95
Grade 4	1-57768-474-5	$7.95
Grade 5	1-57768-475-3	$7.95
Grade 6	1-57768-476-1	$7.95

Certificate of Accomplishment

THIS CERTIFIES THAT

HAS SUCCESSFULLY COMPLETED

Spectrum
Language Arts
Grade 3
WORKBOOK

CONGRATULATIONS AND KEEP UP THE GOOD WORK!

McGraw-Hill
Consumer Products

A Division of The McGraw-Hill Companies

Publisher